1, 2, 3 JOHN AND JUDE

LEARNING AND LIVING THE TRUTH

JUDSON EDWARDS

Annual
Bible
Study

Teaching Guide

SMYTH&HELWYS
PUBLISHING INCORPORATED · MACON GEORGIA

Smyth & Helwys Publishing, Inc.
6316 Peake Road
Macon, Georgia 31210-3960
1-800-747-3016

Library of Congress Catalog-in-Publication Data

Title: 1, 2, 3 John and Jude : learning and living the truth / by Judson
  Edwards.
Description: Macon : Smyth & Helwys, 2017. | Series: Annual Bible study
Identifiers: LCCN 2017039914 | ISBN 9781573129824 (pbk. : alk. paper)
Subjects: LCSH: Bible. Epistles of John--Study and teaching. | Bible.
  Epistles of John--Criticism, interpretation, etc. | Bible. Jude--Study and
  teaching. | Bible. Jude--Criticism, interpretation, etc.
Classification: LCC BS2805.55 .E39 2017 | DDC 227/.9406--dc23
LC record available at https://lccn.loc.gov/2017039914

CONTENTS

)Annual
Bible
Study

P. Keith Gammons
Publisher / Executive Vice
President

Leslie Andres
Editor

Kelley F. Land
Assistant Editor

Katie Brookins
Associate Editor

**Daniel Emerson
Dave Jones**
Graphic Design

1-800-747-3016 (USA)

SMYTH&HELWYS
PUBLISHING INCORPORATED   MACON GEORGIA
WWW.HELWYS.COM

INTRODUCTION: TAPESTRIES OF TRUTH

The first thing I did after agreeing to write this study on 1, 2, and 3 John and Jude was take my Bible to my favorite Starbucks and read those four letters in their entirety. I had read and studied them before, and even preached some sermons from them when I was a pastor, but I needed to refresh my memory. It didn't take long to read all four letters because they have a grand total of eight chapters. After one tall Pike Place coffee, I was finished with my reading.

What struck me as I read those letters was the writers' passion for truth. All four letters focus on learning and living the truth. First John focuses on the truth about loving God, the truth about loving people, and the truth about the difference Jesus makes in a person's life. Second and Third John and Jude all focus on the truth about bad religion and how Christians sometimes must take a stand against bad teaching, bad leading, and bad living within the church.

But the writers of those letters are adamant that their readers should not only know the truth but also contend for the truth and boldly live the truth before others. I left Starbucks convinced that this study needed to be built around their passion for truth. If there is one verse in the Bible that captures the theme of these four letters, it is John 8:32, where Jesus says, "You will know the truth, and the truth will make you free."

After that initial reading at Starbucks, I went home and started rummaging through my books and commentaries for any material I might have on these four letters. In the back of a closet, I discovered an old and long-forgotten study of 1, 2, and 3 John by William Hendricks, the noted Baptist theologian and my former seminary professor. In the introduction to *The Letters of John*, Hendricks wrote,

These three epistles bear a remarkable similarity to one another. Among other things, they are all concerned with truth. They are like cloth cut from the same bolt or like tapestries woven by a single weaver. The subtitle of this study is "Tapestries of Truth," which suggests the closeness of these letters in thought and in their common concern for truth.[1]

Those words confirmed my thoughts about these books. First, Second, and Third John—and Jude as well—are indeed tapestries of truth. To read these old letters is to read the words of people who loved truth, especially the truth they had discovered in the life, death, and resurrection of Jesus Christ. This was the truth they held most dear, the truth that had transformed their lives, and the truth they felt was under attack in the early church.

TRUTH UNDER ATTACK

What, exactly, prompted the writing of these four letters? What motivated these men to start writing so passionately about the truth? They did it because they saw the truth under attack from three specific directions.

First, *they saw the truth under attack by the gnostics*. Gnosticism was a first-century school of thought that believed that matter was evil and spirit was good. This led the gnostics to declare that Jesus could never have been a flesh-and-blood human being, for that physicality would have made him evil. In other words, the gnostics denied Jesus' incarnation because they thought it inconceivable that God would stoop to become a man. This denial of Jesus' humanity meant, among other things, that he hadn't really faced the temptations ordinary humans face and hadn't really died as a human being on a Roman cross.

John, in 1 John, takes on the gnostics at the beginning of his letter: "We declare to you what was from the beginning, what we have heard, what we have seen with our eyes, what we have looked at and touched with our hands, concerning the word of life—this life was revealed, and we have seen it and testify to it . . ." (1:1-2a). In other words, "Make no mistake, gnostics. We have heard, seen, and touched Jesus and know he was a real human being. And now we will tell you why this truth about the incarnation is so vital to the Christian faith."

Second, *they saw the truth under attack by poor church leadership.* In 1 John, John encourages his readers to "test the spirits to see whether they are from God; for many false prophets have gone out into the world" (4:1). Second and Third John speak directly about false teachers in the church and the need for Christians to make sure their leaders are both teaching and living the truth. These writers spoke the truth because they were convinced that many believers in the church were not hearing the truth on a regular basis. In fact, what they were hearing was *untruth.*

Third, they *saw the church under attack by the antinomians.* These were Christians who had perverted the idea of grace and transformed it into complete permissiveness. The antinomians' reasoning was simple: since we're no longer under the law and have been set free by God's grace, we can do anything we want to do. They saw grace as a permission slip to sin or to engage in any kind of immorality that appealed to them. The one-chapter letter of Jude directly addresses the antinomians, pulling no punches in the process.

These writers saw the church at the end of the first century in danger of being seduced by the gnostics, who denied the humanity of Jesus; by poor church leaders, who didn't understand the gospel; and by antinomians, who were preaching that, under grace, anything goes. These falsehoods were egregious enough, they believed, that silence was unacceptable. Someone needed to step up and speak a word of truth, and that is exactly what they did.

TAKING UP PEN AND PAPYRUS

Who were these truth-tellers who wrote 1, 2, 3 John and Jude? That depends on which Bible scholar you happen to read. When it comes to the five letters in the Bible often attributed to the apostle John (1, 2, and 3 John plus the Gospel of John and Revelation), there are five common views about the authorship of these books:

- All five books were written by one man, likely the apostle John.
- Revelation was written by one man, but the other four were written by a different man.
- Revelation was written by one man; the Gospel of John and 1 John were written by another man; and 2 and 3 John were written by a third author.

- Revelation was written by one author, the Gospel by another author, and the three epistles by a third author.
- The thought of all five works is based on the life and thought of one man, the apostle John, and was recorded and transmitted by those who knew and loved him and accurately preserved his teachings.

John the Evangelist

Saint John the Evangelist and his symbol. Second half of 12th C. Elephant ivory, Louvre, Paris, France. (Credit: Jean-Gilles Berizzi. Réunion des Musées Nationaux / Art Resource, NY)

For my part, I'm in the last camp and ascribe all these teachings to the apostle John or one of his close disciples. Even if John didn't write all five books, his thoughts are accurately and faithfully expressed in them. As for the three Johannine epistles in this study, they carry the thinking and spirit of the apostle John, and we can assume that we are in the presence of one of the great minds and spirits in Christian history.

The authorship of Jude is also in question among scholars. There are five people named Judas mentioned in the New Testament, and the most likely candidate for authorship among them is Judas, the brother of Jesus (Matt 13:55; Mark 6:3). In the first verse of his letter, Jude introduces himself as "the servant of Jesus Christ and brother of James." Since James was Jesus' brother, it is reasonable to infer that the writer of Jude was Judas, the brother of both James and Jesus.

If our authorship designations happen to be correct, we are sitting at the feet of two very credible teachers. If John the apostle wrote, or at least inspired, the three Johannine epistles, and if Judas the brother of Jesus wrote Jude, we are studying under people who knew Jesus well and loved him dearly.

If anybody deserves our respect and attention, it's these two men.

EXPLORING THE TRUTH

Here's the outline we will use in studying the way John and Jude explore the truth in these letters.

I. The Truth about Loving God (1 John 1:1–3:10)
    A. Get Focused (1:1-4)
    B. Get Real (1:5–2:2)
    C. Get Busy (2:3-14)
    D. Get Eccentric (2:15-29)
    E. Get Challenged (3:1-10)

II. The Truth about Loving People (1 John 3:11–4:21)
    A. Get Personal (3:11-24)
    B. Get Smart (4:1-6)
    C. Get Motivated (4:7-21)

III. The Truth about the Difference Jesus Makes (1 John 5:1-21)
    A. The Reason for Our Victory (5:1-5)
    B. The Source of Our Life (5:6-12)
    C. The Cause of Our Confidence (5:13-17)
    D. The Key to Our Understanding (5:18-21)

IV. The Truth about Bad Religion (2 & 3 John, Jude)
    A. Bad Teaching (2 John)
    B. Bad Leading (3 John)
    C. Bad Living (Jude)

WHATEVER HAPPENED TO TRUTH?

As we study these letters and move through this outline, we will have ample opportunity to consider our own truth. Reading these four explorations of truth will enable us to consider the truth by which we live, the truth that guides our decisions, the truth that gives us hope and joy. Furthermore, we will be able to consider not only the truths that undergird our lives but also the nature of truth itself. Is there objective truth that exists outside of us? And is there divine truth that has come from God to guide us as we live?

John and Jude certainly believed in objective, divine truth, but people in our day are not so sure. Nearly thirty years ago, Walter Truett Anderson wrote a book about postmodernism that he called *Reality Isn't What It Used to Be*. He began the book with this observation:

> In recent decades we have passed, like Alice slipping through the looking glass, into a new world. This postmodern world looks and feels in many ways like the modern world that preceded it: we still have the belief systems of premodern societies. If there is anything we have plenty of it is belief systems. But we also have something else: a growing suspicion that all belief systems— all ideas about human reality—are social constructions.[2]

In other words, all belief systems are created by human beings searching for meaning. In the postmodern world, *subjective* truth has replaced *objective* truth. What is true for me may not be true for you and vice versa. It's a "different-strokes-for-different-folks" kind of world, and change and flexibility are the orders of the day. Anderson continues:

> Like hermit crabs who skitter about in the tide pools wearing the shells of dead snails, we don old belief systems that do not always fit too well, and go about our business. Most of us now are not so much believers as possessors of beliefs. Conversion comes easy and often. The seeker after religious faith tries not one religion, but any number of them . . . . In the collapse of belief, a thousand sub-cultures bloom, and new belief systems arrive as regularly as the daily mail.[3]

Anderson's assessment of our culture appears right on target to me, which means people like John and Jude seem dogmatic and authoritarian to us. They were not postmodern people by any stretch, and they most definitely were believers rather than merely possessors of beliefs. As we study their writings, we may want to question some of the truths they espouse, but we may also want to question some of the ways we now process and understand truth. If we have the courage, we may even want to question whether we're truly Christian believers . . . or just possessors of Christian beliefs.

FLYING UPSIDE DOWN

Dallas Willard begins his book *The Divine Conspiracy* with this illustration:

> Recently a pilot was practicing high-speed maneuvers in a jet fighter. She turned the controls for what she thought was a steep ascent—and flew straight into the ground. She was unaware that she had been flying upside-down.
>
> This is a parable of human existence in our times—not exactly that everyone is crashing, though there is enough of that—but most of us as individuals, and world society as a whole, live at high speed, and often with no clue whether we are flying upside down or right-side up. Indeed, we are haunted by a strong suspicion that there may be no difference—or at least that it is unknown or irrelevant.[4]

How do we know if we're flying upside down or right-side up? Who, or what, can tell us? Christians have always believed that the Bible is the best source for determining the answer to that all-important question. In the Bible, we learn how to fly right-side up—and what to do if we discover if we're flying upside down. In the Bible we learn God's truth, a truth that can set us free to live with joy and to be all that God created us to be.

The four short letters we will study here are consumed with the idea of helping us fly right-side up. They want us to learn the truth and then live that truth in specific, practical ways. So we will study 1, 2, and 3 John and Jude to learn the truth about loving God, the truth about loving people, the truth about the difference Jesus makes in our lives, and the truth about bad religion.

Perhaps we can think of these four studies as a crash course in how not to crash.

THE PLAN FOR THIS TEACHING GUIDE

Our study of 1, 2, 3 John and Jude will be divided into four sessions that will survey the four truths I've just mentioned:

Session 1: The Truth about Loving God (1 John 1:1–3:10). As we study the first part of 1 John, we will focus on what John tells us about loving God. We will discover that loving God involves getting focused, getting real, getting busy, getting eccentric, and getting challenged. In this session, we will sit at the feet of the "disciple whom Jesus loved" and let him teach us the truth about loving God.

Session 2: The Truth about Loving People (1 John 3:11–4:21). These two chapters in 1 John will focus our attention on loving the people around us. We will discover that, according to John, loving people involves getting personal, getting smart, and getting motivated.

Session 3: The Truth about the Difference Jesus Makes (1 John 5:1-21). The final chapter in 1 John celebrates the truth of Jesus Christ—who he is and the difference he makes in people's lives. Since 1 John was written against the backdrop of Gnosticism and its false claims about Jesus, it is not surprising that John ends his letter with a resounding statement of bold Christology. He says that Christ is the reason for our victory, the source of our life, the cause of our confidence, and the key to our understanding. In this session, we will celebrate the difference Jesus makes in our lives and in the lives of all who declare him Lord.

Session 4: The Truth about Bad Religion (2 & 3 John, Jude). This final session will examine these three one-chapter letters that all address the issue of bad religion. As we study 2 John, we will learn about bad teaching in the early church. As we study 3 John, we will learn about bad leadership that was evident in at least one of those churches. And as we study Jude, we will learn about bad living, as certain Christians were distorting the idea of grace and ignoring the ethical and moral demands of the gospel. This final session will remind us that not all religion is good, that religion can even become evil and life-destroying, and that Christians must always contend for the truth that leads to abundant living.

This teaching guide also includes suggestions for worship and preaching for those churches that would like to build their worship services around the themes of the study.

SUGGESTIONS FOR WORSHIP AND PREACHING

An Order of Worship

This first suggested worship service is for churches that will launch this study with one service focusing on the four letters. The service is built around the first four verses in 1 John, where John declares that he has heard, seen, and touched Jesus and wants his readers to know it.

Set against the backdrop of Gnosticism, which denied the humanity of Christ, John's letter is a ringing endorsement of the truth about Jesus, the friend he knew so well and the one who had changed his life so dramatically.

The Worship of God
". . . this life was revealed, and we have seen it and testify to it." (1 John 1:2a)

Spoken Call to Worship
The Chiming of the Hour
Processional Hymn: "All Hail the Power of Jesus' Name!"
Responsive Reading
    Leader: As the hand is made for holding and the eye for seeing . . .
    Congregation: You have fashioned me for joy.
    Leader: Share with me the vision that shall find it everywhere:
    Congregation: In the wild violet's beauty;
    Leader: In the lark's melody;
    Congregation: In the face of a steadfast person;
    Leader: In a child's smile;
    Congregation: In a mother's love;
    All: In the life and spirit of Jesus the Christ. (*A Gaelic Prayer*)
Choral Meditation: "God So Loved the World" (Dan & Heidi Goeller, copyright 2006 by Dan Goeller Music)
Pastoral Prayer

Hymn: "O Love That Wilt Not Let Me Go"
Receiving Tithes and Offerings
Singing of the Doxology
Word of the Lord: 1 John 1:1-4
    Worship Leader: This is the Word of the Lord.
    Congregation: Thanks be to God.
Anthem: "With Every Breath" (Ken Medema, copyright 1993 by Shawnee
Press)
Sermon: "Detours on the Journey of Faith"
Hymn of Response: "Shine, Jesus, Shine"
Choral Benediction: "Yours Is the Kingdom" (Cindy Berry, copyright 1999 by
Shawnee Press)
Postlude

A Sermon Sketch

"Detours on the Journey of Faith" (1 John 1:1-4)

Introduction
"Follow me." With those two words, Jesus revolutionized the lives of some
men in the first century. Those men did choose to follow him, and their lives
were changed forever. When they followed Jesus, old things passed away and all
things became new.

That word "follow" literally meant "to share the same road," and that is
precisely what Peter, James, John, and all the other disciples did after they
accepted Jesus' invitation. They shared the same road as Jesus, saw him love and
laugh and cry, and learned the meaning of life from him.

Since then, Christians have understood that following Jesus means sharing
the road with him. It means we go on a journey, that we're always moving and
changing, and that to journey with Jesus is to discover new truth all along the
way.

From time to time, we Christian pilgrims need to stop and ask ourselves
some questions: Are we changing? Are we learning? Are we loving more than
we used to love? Are we getting more depth and substance to our faith? Are we
moving or standing still?

Today we begin a study of four short letters in the New Testament that
were all written to help Christians grow and move. The writers of 1, 2, 3 John

and Jude were obsessed with truth, and they wanted the early Christians to be obsessed with truth as well. They wrote these brief letters to help those Christians learn and live the truth.

Two specific problems were in the backdrop of these letters, and John and Jude spoke to both of them. As the early Christians moved along on their journey with Christ, they encountered two detours that threatened to sidetrack them. Since these detours are still around in our day, we would do well to hear what John and Jude say about them. We will focus specifically in this service on the first four verses in 1 John as John tries to get his readers off the detours and back on the road of knowing and following Christ.

The Doctrinal Detour

The first detour those early Christians had to deal with was a doctrinal one. Gnosticism was a growing threat in the early church, and it prompted all four of the letters we will be studying. The gnostics believed, among other things, that Jesus wasn't a real human being. Since they believed that anything material and physical was inherently evil, they decided that Jesus couldn't have been human. That's why John is so adamant in the opening verses of 1 John. He wanted his readers to know that he had heard, seen, and touched Jesus himself, that he was an eyewitness to the humanity of Christ.

Gnosticism is no longer a menacing threat to the church, but we still have some doctrinal detours to deal with. Perhaps the most glaring one is the notion that truth itself no longer exists. Our culture increasingly believes that all truth is subjective, that we each must cobble together a truth that works for us. There's nothing "out there" that is true; it's all "in here." The modern mentality questions the very existence of Christian doctrine and deems it presumptuous and dogmatic. In other words, John and Jude would have a hard time drawing a crowd in modern America.

The Disillusionment Detour

The other detour beckoning to those early Christians was disillusionment. These four letters were all written at end of the first century, which meant that their readers were the children and grandchildren of the first Christians.

Some major questions and doubts were starting to creep into their minds: Is all this true, this gospel about Jesus and his Way? Why hasn't Jesus returned as he promised? How can we know which brand of Christianity is true anyway?

And how can we have the passion of our ancestors when we haven't heard what they heard or seen what they saw?

If those questions sound remarkably current and relevant to us, if we also grapple with disillusionment from time to time, these old letters can give us some help. John and Jude wrote their letters to counter both the doctrinal detour presented by the gnostics and the disillusionment detour presented by the passing of time.

Conclusion

Most of us here this morning, at some point, have responded to Jesus' call to follow him. Whether it happened seventy years ago or just yesterday, we decided to get on the road with Jesus and journey through life with him.

If we have been on this journey for a while, we have learned that there is no shortage of detours along the Way. And the two detours that prompted the writing of 1, 2, 3 John and Jude are still around today. We still have *content* issues to deal with as we decide what to believe and what we consider to be true. And we also have *emotional* issues to deal with as we decide how to stay motivated and passionate in our faith.

One thing we know for certain is that "follow me" from Jesus is not something we hear just one time. It's something we hear every day of our lives. And staying off the detours is a constant challenge.

NOTES

1. William Hendricks, *The Letters of John* (Nashville: Convention Press, 1970) 5–6.

2. Walter Truett Anderson, *Reality Isn't What It Used to Be* (San Francisco: Harper & Row, 1990) 3.

3. Ibid., 9–10.

4. Dallas Willard, *The Divine Conspiracy* (New York: HarperCollins, 1998) 1–2.

THE TRUTH ABOUT LOVING GOD

Focal Text—1 John 1:1–3:10

Once upon a time, the Christian community in Ephesus was in trouble. The trouble didn't come from outside their community—no Babylonians or Romans were persecuting them—but from inside. The first threat came from within the church community; the second threat came from within the lives of individual Christians. The first threat was doctrinal; the second threat was emotional.

The first threat had to do with the gnostics, a group of people inside the church whose teaching about Christ was contrary to the gospel. The gnostics

Map of Asia Minor

believed the world was black and white. That is, anything material or physical was inherently evil, and anything ethereal or spiritual was inherently holy. Body and creation were bad; church and spirit were good. This dichotomy led them to say that Jesus couldn't have had a real body because that would have made him evil. He may have looked like a man, talked like a man, and lived like a man, but he wasn't *really* a man. In short, the gnostics denied the humanity of Jesus and, in the process, caused quite a controversy in the early church. First John and several other New Testament letters were written to confront the tenets of the gnostics.

The second threat was a personal one that affected each person in the church in Ephesus. Many in that church were growing disillusioned and doubtful. Since 1 John was written at the end of the first century, these people were the children and grandchildren of the first Christians. They were starting to wonder about the truth of the Christian gospel and had some serious, unsettling questions: Is this true, this story told us by our parents and grandparents? Why hasn't Jesus returned as he promised? With all the new brands of Christianity popping up, who knows what to believe anymore? Is there some way to tell true expressions of faith from false ones? Is there some way to get back to the essence of it all? And is there some way to recapture the spirit and passion of our ancestors?

A *doctrinal* threat and a *disillusionment* threat were causing tremors in the church in Ephesus at the end of the first century, and the Christians there needed some guidance. Thankfully—for them and for us—there came a word to them from one of the true spiritual giants, a man who both knew and loved them. They received a letter from the apostle John, or at least one of John's disciples, that spoke directly to their dilemma. John took on their doctrinal questions as well as their disillusionment questions, and he tried to give them some practical help.

That is good news for us because it means we have at our fingertips an old manual of personal renewal that has been used for centuries. Should we have questions about who Jesus is, or should we start to doubt our faith, we have a trusty manual of renewal that Christians have turned to for a long time. When we need clarity about the nature of God, or when we need a second wind in our spiritual journey, we don't have to invent a plan of renewal, probe self-help books, or tune in to the latest guru on television. We already have what we need, tucked away in the pages of the Bible. First John is the manual of personal renewal we need, and it begins with John's counsel on the truth about loving God.

GET FOCUSED (1:1-4)

First John has an odd beginning. It has no introduction, no mention of the writer or the recipients, and no "Hi, how are you, it's been a while since we've seen each other." Instead, John immediately brings Jesus on stage and shines the spotlight on him. It's as if John is saying, "This is not going to be a letter about me, or even about you, but about him. If you are going to deal with your confusion and your disillusionment, you will have to get focused on Jesus." From the beginning of the letter, we get the idea that loving God means focusing on Jesus Christ.

That has always been the case for Christians. The way of personal renewal, the way to love and serve God, is to focus on Christ. Too often, the essence of the Christian Way gets lost in a pile of religious stuff that doesn't matter very much. Layers of religious detritus—boring worship services, interminable committee meetings, silly church fights, long-winded preachers, syrupy music, heated doctrinal disputes, and dozens of other things—start to pile up in our lives. We eventually have so many layers of religious stuff in our lives that we forget the essence of it all. As with an old house my parents once owned, we have so many layers of carpeting on our souls that we've forgotten the pristine wood floors underneath.

What John tries to do in 1 John is remove those layers and get us back to the heart of the gospel: focusing on Christ and letting him instruct and inspire us. When we do that, we remember at least three things about who Jesus was.

First, *Jesus was profound.* We tend to overlook this characteristic of Jesus. Jesus had a brilliant mind. Dallas Willard reminds us of this in *The Divine Conspiracy:*

> Can we seriously imagine that Jesus could be Lord and not be smart? If he were divine would he be dumb? Or uninformed? Once you stop to think about it, how could he be what we take him to be in all other respects and not be the best-informed and most intelligent person of all, the smartest person who ever lived?[1]

But still we are prone to seek out other experts when we need personal renewal:

> Strangely, we seem prepared to learn how to live from almost anyone but
> him. We are ready to believe that the latest studies have more to teach us
> about love and sex than he does, and that Louis Rukeyser knows more about
> finances. Dear Abby can teach us more about how to get along with our family
> members and co-workers, and Carl Sagan is a better authority on the cosmos.
> We lose any sense of the difference between information and wisdom, and act
> accordingly.[2]

Let us celebrate together the wisdom and brilliance of Jesus the Nazarene. He
truly was profound, and his teachings have weathered the test of time.

Second, *Jesus was practical.* The brilliance of Jesus is that he was both
profound *and* practical. He wasn't complicated and didn't deal with esoteric
topics. He used simple words to address essential issues. Think, for example,
about the Sermon on the Mount. In three biblical chapters, he addressed a
multitude of life's most pressing concerns, and he did it both briefly and bril-
liantly. No wonder the people of his day said he spoke as one with authority
and not as the scribes and Pharisees. He spoke on relevant issues, and they
could understand what he said.

That's why we can still turn to Jesus when we want answers to the real
questions of life. He spoke about the very issues that concern us most, and we
continue to discover how practical his teachings are two thousand years after he
spoke them.

Third, *Jesus was personal.* He wasn't concerned about movements, causes,
and popularity polls. He was concerned about individuals. He had eyes for
individual people: the woman at the well, Zaccheus, little children, blind
Bartimaeus, the rich ruler, the thief on the cross, and countless others. As the
Gospels unfurl, they reveal a series of encounters between Jesus and individuals.
These individual encounters help explain why his disciples didn't understand
him. They were thinking movements, numbers, offerings, and politics. They
were thinking institutionally, and Jesus was thinking personally—and never the
twain would meet.

When we focus on the life and ministry of Jesus, his attention to individual
people is one of the things that jumps out at us. He loved individual people,

spoke to individual people, and met the needs of individual people. He would have been a terrible politician, but he was a wonderful Savior.

As we begin our study of 1 John, I remind you of these three qualities because John wants us to focus on Jesus: "This life appeared; we have seen it and testify to it, and we proclaim to you eternal life, which was with the Father, and has appeared to us" (1:2). As we focus on Jesus' life, we hope to become transformed into his image and become more profound, practical, and personal ourselves.

In 1850, Nathaniel Hawthorne wrote a short story titled "The Great Stone Face." A great stone face was carved into a mountain. One gentle soul named Ernest became so enamored by that stone face that he went daily to gaze at it. At the end of the story, towns-people noticed that Ernest had changed over the years, that both his appearance and his spirit had been transformed into the image of the great stone face he had stared at every day of his life.

John begins 1 John by having us focus our attention on Jesus, hoping that in doing so we will be transformed into his image.

Beginnings

Note that in Johannine thought, great interest centers on beginnings, a pivotal concept, whether it has to do with a pre-creational existence (John 1:1; cf. Heb 1:10), the historical ministry of Jesus (John 8:25; 15:27; 16:4; cf. Acts 1:21-22; Phil 4:15), or the outset of discipleship (1 John 2:7, 24; 3:11; 2 John 5; 6). The author's appeal to authority depends particularly upon the teaching (commandments) of Jesus and consistency with the instruction given to the recipients. He refers not to the beginning of time but to the beginning of the community.

GET REAL (1:5–2:2)

Beginning with verse 5, John starts to write about getting real. If we are to love God, he says, we must be totally honest. We can't play games with God and expect the relationship to have any meaning. In these verses, he mentions two games the Christians of the first century must have been fond of playing—two games, I think you will agree, that we modern Christians still play from time to time.

One game John mentions we might call *charades*—the attempt to look Christian without really being Christian. John describes the charades game like this: "God is light, in him there is no darkness at all. If we say that we have fellowship with him while we are walking in darkness, we lie and do not do what is true; but if we walk in the light as he himself is in the light, we have fellowship with one another, and the blood of Jesus his son cleanses us from all sin" (1:5b-6).

In charades, we play a role, trying to look pious and religious while never being changed on the inside. John is describing here the age-old discrepancy between words and actions. It's one thing to say we're followers of Christ; it's another thing altogether to adopt Jesus' priorities and try to live the way he lived.

That's why Frederick Buechner, in *Wishful Thinking*, wrote, "Generally speaking, if you want to know who you really are as distinct from who you like to think you are, keep an eye on where your feet take you."[3] Our lips may lie, but our feet don't. Our walk says much more than our talk. As the adage rightfully says, "Who we are speaks so loudly people can hardly hear what we say."

This was no new truth John was telling the Ephesian Christians, but he wasn't really trying to give them new truth. They were already besieged by new truth from the culture outside the church and from the gnostics inside the church. John was reminding those Christians of *old* truth, basic stuff that will always be true. He was saying, "Get real, and start to live what you claim to believe."

That is always a good word, but it seems especially appropriate for our day. Contemporary American culture is a "talk/image/façade" kind of culture. As one television ad reminded us, "Image is everything." What matters most in our world is the package. We tend to value style over substance, personality over character, body over soul, and popularity over truth.

In that kind of culture, it is natural, even expected, to play charades. What is crucial, even in the church, is how we sound, how we look, the image we project. Psychologist Erich Fromm once said the dominant personality character in our culture is the "marketing character" who packages himself or herself to be appealing to the highest bidder. The marketing character is constantly changing to meet the demands of the market.

Jesus used a graphic word to describe this approach to life: "hypocrite." That word literally means "a mask-wearer." It describes one playing a game, adopting a role or image to try to impress others. When Jesus used the word, he was describing the most religious and respected men in his society, the scribes and Pharisees. They looked and sounded great to everyone around them, but Jesus said there were simply playing charades.

That seems to be exactly what John is referring to in these verses. He saw people saying one thing and doing another, claiming to be people of light while blatantly walking in the darkness. He wanted his Ephesian readers to get real and start *walking* more than *talking*.

The second game he describes in these verses could be called *denial*. He mentions this game twice, in verses 8 and 10:

- "If we say we that have no sin, we deceive ourselves, and the truth is not in us."
- "If we say that we have not sinned, we make him a liar, and his word is not in us."

One could make a strong case that denial is the oldest game in history. In the garden of Eden, Adam denied any wrongdoing and blamed Eve. Then Eve denied any wrongdoing and blamed the serpent. Then the serpent looked around . . . and couldn't find anyone else to blame! The denial game is as old as the creation story and as modern as today's newspaper.

A writer named Charles Sykes wrote a provocative book titled *A Nation of Victims*. He began the book like this:

> Something extraordinary is happening in American society. Criss-crossed by invisible trip-wires of emotional, racial, sexual, and psychological grievance, American life is increasingly characterized by the plaintive insistence, "I am a victim." The victimization of American life is remarkably egalitarian. From the addicts of South Bronx to the self-styled emotional roadkills of Manhattan's Upper East Side, the mantra of the victims is the same: "I am not responsible; it's not my fault."[4]

A British newspaper looked at our culture and noted with bemusement: "If you lose your job, you can sue for the mental distress of being fired. If your bank goes broke, the government has insured your deposits. If you drive drunk and crash, you can sue somebody for failing to warn you to stop drinking. There is always somebody else to blame."[5]

That sounds remarkably like Adam and Eve in the garden, doesn't it? It also sounds like the denial game John describes in 1 John. If we say we have no sin, he says, we're fooling ourselves. We're also making God a liar because God knows the truth about us and has declared us hopeless without a Savior. But still we keep trying to play the denial game and singing at the top of our lungs, "It's *them*, it's *them*, it's *them*, O Lord, standin' in the need of prayer."

John's advice? Get real. Be honest. We have sinned and fallen short of the glory of God. But "if we confess our sins, he who is faithful and just will forgive our sins and cleanse us from all unrighteousness" (2:9). We can keep playing the denial game if we choose, but the price we pay is a high one. In pretending to be sinless and perfect, we never understand the grace of God that accepts us even at our worst. We keep playing a dishonest game when an honest admission of our sin will enable us to experience forgiveness and freedom. We don't have to pretend anymore, John says. We can come out of the closet, admit our sin, and splash in amazing grace.

I once saw a church with an intriguing name: Church of the Holy Innocents. I thought to myself that if you have to be holy and innocent to be part of that church, membership will be pretty low! But we would still like to think of ourselves that way—as holy, innocent people sailing above the imperfections of ordinary humans. We've "got it all together." We're doing fine, thank you very much. Save your sermons on sin for those who need them.

John wants us to get real and look honestly at our lives. When we do that, we have to confess our sin, but we also get to see something (or Someone) wonderful: "We have an advocate with the Father, Jesus Christ, the righteous; and he is the atoning sacrifice for our sins, and not for ours only but for the sins of the whole world" (2:2).

When we get real and get honest, we can no longer declare ourselves to be holy and innocent. We get to declare ourselves to be something even more remarkable: sinful and forgiven.

Confession of Sin in the New Testament

Not so prevalent as one might imagine, we find an account of (1) people responding to the preaching of the Baptizer by confessing their sins (Mark 1:4, 5), (2) people in Ephesus confessing in response to the Pauline mission (Acts 19:18), and (3) in the context of healing, James admonishing Christians to confess their sins but to one another (Jas 5:16). The confessing of Christ appears rather often in the New Testament and also in 1 John (2:23; 4:2, 15).

GET BUSY (2:3-14)

Before we look at these verses from 1 John, I want to direct your attention to the morning newspaper and talk about the nature of news. When we read the newspaper, we are reading three kinds of news that affects us in three different ways.

First, there is *informational news,* news that informs us and gives us facts. Most of the news in the morning paper is informational news. We learn how the stock market did yesterday, what's showing at the local theater, what the president said in his cabinet meeting, and whether our favorite baseball team won or lost. Informational news affects our heads—what we know.

Second, there is *emotional news,* news that moves beyond facts and makes us feel something. Sometimes informational news becomes emotional news. If our stock plummets, that news sends our spirits plummeting as well. If our favorite team got beat last night, that news might upset us. Certainly, if we read in the obituary section that someone we know died, that news weighs heavy on our hearts. Informational news affects our heads; emotional news affects our hearts—how we feel.

Third, there is *personal news.* In just about every issue of the paper there is something that goes beyond our thinking and feeling to make us behave differently. For example, if the paper says it's going to rain, we'll decide to take our raincoat to work. If an article describes the effect of bacon on our arteries, we might change our breakfast menu. If we read that a store is having a big sale, we might decide to go by that store on our way home from work. When something we read in the morning paper changes our behavior, we have read personal news that affects what we do, not just what we know or feel.

I hope this will help us put these verses in 1 John into perspective. John was writing news to Christians in Ephesus who were dealing with the gnostic heresy and with some disillusionment in their own faith. He wanted to give them "second wind," to remind them about the wonder of Christ and the indispensability of their faith in him. He invited them to get focused on Christ in 1:1-4, then to get real and quit playing games with God in 1:5–2:2. Now, in 2:3-14, he invites them to get busy. In other words, he wants the news he is telling them to be personal news—not just news they know and feel but news they translate into action.

Here's the heart of his message: "Now by this we may be sure that we know him, if we obey his commandments. Whoever says, 'I have come to know him,' but does not obey his commandments, is a liar, and in such a person the truth does not exist; but whoever obeys his word, truly in this person the love of God has reached perfection. By this we may be sure that we are in him: whoever says, 'I abide in him,' ought to walk as he walked" (2:3-6).

John is saying, "Obey. Walk as he walked. Get busy. Have enough evidence in your life that you could be convicted of being a Christian." Behind that admonition to get busy were some competing concepts of religious news that the people in Ephesus were hearing:

- The gnostics. Theirs was an informational view of religion. Just know the doctrines, understand the concepts, and think your way to God. The word "gnosis" means "knowledge" in Greek. The gnostics saw themselves as the religious elite, the ones who knew the secret codes that enabled them to unlock the mysteries about God. For them, a relationship with God began with the head.
- The mystery religions. Theirs was an emotional view of religion and truth. The gnostics may have had secret knowledge about God, but the adherents of the mystery religions had secret experiences with God. William Barclay described their religion like this: "Everything was designed to heighten the emotional atmosphere. There was cunning lighting; sensuous music; perfumed incense; a marvelous liturgy . . . . This was not so much *knowing* God as *feeling* God."[6] For the mystery religions, a relationship with God began with the heart.

But John, in these verses, challenges the gnostics' concept of *knowing* and the mystery religions' concept of *feeling* to declare the gospel's concept of *doing*. Gospel news is not informational or emotional; it is personal. And until gospel news affects the way we live, until it motivates us to obey God, we don't have the real thing.

There are three distinct sections in this passage:

- *Walk as Jesus walked (vv. 3-6).* They will know we are followers of Christ by what we do, not by what we think or feel. We are his followers only if we walk in his footsteps.

- *Love the brothers and sisters (vv. 7-11)*. In the next session of this study, we will focus on the truth about loving people (3:11–4:21). But here John alludes to the truth he will elucidate later in the letter: no one can truly love God without also truly loving people. Those two realities are inseparable.
- *A poetic postscript (vv. 12-14)*. John offers blessings to some different segments of the church: the little children, the fathers, and the young people. He commends all these groups for their faithfulness.

When Jesus stood before Pilate, Pilate asked him, "What is truth?" (Jn 18:38). The gnostics would have said, "Truth is something you know." The mystery religions would have said, "Truth is something you feel." But John would have said, "Truth is something you do."

About twenty years ago, a small, secretive group was working on what they called "The Second Coming Project." They saw cloning technology as an opportunity to bring Jesus literally back to earth. Their plan was to obtain a small DNA sample from one of the Christian relics that include a piece of Jesus' body—a drop of blood or strand of hair from something like the shroud of Turin. They hoped to place this cloned fetus into a woman's womb and let her carry him to birth. The birth was tentatively scheduled for December 25, 2001.

Those working on "The Second Coming Project" had high hopes. They hoped their plan would bring world peace and usher in a new and wonderful society. They knew, of course, that there were problems. Were those religious relics even authentic? Was it possible to clone a 2000-year-old DNA sample? They knew it would be a miracle if they pulled it off. And, sure enough, the miracle never happened. December 25, 2001, came and went and Jesus wasn't reborn.

How does Jesus get into the world anyway? If he can't be cloned from relics, how does he come? We've known the answer for a long time. He comes into the world through his people, through us—the people who know and obey him. The world sees Jesus through the people who walk the way he walked and love the way he loved.

That's what John wanted those Ephesian Christians to remember. Get busy, and walk the way he walked. Get busy, and love the way he loved. This news of the gospel is more than informational and emotional; it's personal. And it changes the way we live.

GET ECCENTRIC (2:15-29)

My dictionary defines the word "eccentric" like this: "deviating from the norm, as in conduct; odd; whimsical; peculiar; unconventional." But the first definition it gives is "not having the same center; having different centers, as two circles."

The Christian life, then, is the eccentric life. When we make our pledge to Christ, we get a new center. Old things pass away, and all things become new. We're catapulted into a different system with new priorities, attitudes, and dreams. In Christ, we become eccentrics.

Walter Wink has written a book titled *Engaging the Powers* in which he calls the world's way of doing things "the domination system," as opposed to God's way of doing things, which is the kingdom of God. Nowhere in the Bible is the contrast more clearly delineated than in Jesus' Sermon on the Mount. That sermon is a manifesto for eccentrics and delineates specific ways the Christian rejects "the domination system" to embrace the kingdom of God.

Read carefully through the Sermon on the Mount and you will notice at least fifteen different "turnings," fifteen ways the follower of Jesus is to be an eccentric. It begins with the Beatitudes, a strange, paradoxical description of happiness, and ends with Jesus talking about a broad road, a narrow road, a house built on sand, and a house built on rock. It's obvious when you get to the end of the Sermon on the Mount that anyone who takes Jesus seriously is a true eccentric, walking a different road and building on a different foundation.

These verses in 1 John remind us of that same truth: "Do not love the world or the things in the world. The love of the Father is not in those who love the world; for all that is in the world—the desire of the flesh, the desire of the eyes, the pride in riches—comes not from the Father but from the world. And the world and its desires are passing away, but those who do the will of God live forever" (2:15-17).

When John uses the word "world" in those verses, he is not talking about trees and hills and wind. He is talking

The Hostile Environment of the World

Elsewhere the Epistle realistically takes notes of the hostile environment in the world for the Christian (4:1-6), and in John the evangelist announces that the Advocate will prove the world wrong about sin and righteousness (16:8). Believers do not belong to the world (17:14, 16) and should not act as they do. The epistolary writer does not expect the believers to remove themselves from the world—presuming familiarity with 17:15. But he enjoins his readers to conquer (2:14), to overcome the world through faith (5:4-5), sharing in the victory of Christ (cf. 16:33).

about "the domination system," with its desire of the flesh, desire of the eyes, and pride in riches. The world, as John depicts it, is full of self and self's desires. In the world's system, everything revolves around me, and everyone wants to be rich and famous.

The poet Naomi Nye has written a poem about being famous that defines fame more along the lines of God's kingdom:

> The river is famous to the fish.
> The loud voice is famous to silence
> Which knew it would inherit the earth
> Before anybody said so.
> The cat sleeping on the fence is famous
> To the birds watching him from the birdhouse.
> The tear is famous, briefly, to the cheek.
> The idea you carry close to your bosom
> Is famous to your bosom.
> The boot is famous to the earth,
> More famous than the dress shoe,
> Which is famous only to floors.
> The bent photograph is famous to the one
> Who carries it and not at all famous to the one who is pictured.
> I want to be famous to shuffling men
> Who smile while crossing the streets,
> Sticky children in grocery lines,
> Famous as the one who smiled back.
> I want to be famous in the way a pulley is
> Famous, or a buttonhole, not because
> It did anything spectacular, but because
> It never forgot what it could do.[7]

John was reminding those Christians in Ephesus that there was a whole system out there tempting them to leave the kingdom of God and the way of Jesus, tempting them to become famous in the wrong way, to lust and boast and crave more. John calls the proponents of this system "the antichrists."

There is in our day—among certain Christians anyway—a passion to study the antichrist, to try to pinpoint who he is and when he is coming. John speaks about the antichrist in a different way, though. He sees not one antichrist coming at the end of time but many antichrists among us now, tempting us to forsake the way of Jesus to join "the domination system." For John, the antichrist is more a mindset or spirit than a historical figure. The antichrist is any person enamored with this world and tempting us to forget the other one.

John's remedy for fighting off the temptations of the antichrists around us is captured in one word: "abide." He uses that word six times in verses 24-28.

In the Midst of Turmoil and Lust, Man Is Carried off by Death

Alfred Rethel. *In the midst of Turmoil and Lust, Man is Carried off by Death.* Kupferstichkabinett, Staatliche Kunstsammlungen, Dresden, Germany. (Credit: Erich Lessing / Art Resource, NY)

The 19th C. German artist Alfred Rethel produced several depictions of death. In this work, Death brings an end to those who are caught up in the lusts of this world (cf. 1 Jn 2:16-17).

We are to abide in Christ, abide in what we heard from the beginning, abide in the eccentric truth that put us on a narrow road in the first place.

Most of us have probably heard the famous quote from Thoreau's *Walden* about stepping to the beat of different drummer. But long before Thoreau wrote those words, John said the same thing to the Christians in Ephesus at the end of the first century. They were stepping to the beat of a Different Drummer. They were eccentrics, and John didn't want them to forget it.

When I was a boy, I became enamored with learning how to stand on my head. I wanted to do handstands but wasn't strong enough and had to settle for headstands. I practiced and practiced and got pretty good at it. I got to where I could do a headstand for several minutes without losing my balance. I still remember how different the world looked upside down.

I realize now that it was good training for becoming a Christian. Perhaps we should include a session on standing on your head in vacation Bible school and children's Sunday school classes in our churches. We could teach the kids to stand on their heads and then tell them that Jesus took the world's truth and stood it on its head. We could tell them that Jesus calls us to look at life upside down.

That's what this passage in 1 John is about. John wanted the early Christians to remember the difference to which they had been called. And, as we study this passage, we know that it applies to us as well. We are called to be eccentrics. We read 1 John and remember our marching orders: "Do not love the world or the things in the world. The love of the Father is not in those who love the world" (2:15).

We've dropped out of the domination system to establish the kingdom of God. And we've decided to become famous to those old men shuffling across the street.

GET CHALLENGED (3:1-10)

My first experience with sailing was a disaster. A friend and I rented a sailboat one day and spent the afternoon sailing on Clear Lake, near Houston. Never mind that neither one of us had ever been in a sailboat before. How hard can it be to sit in a boat and let the wind blow you around a lake?

Well, we were to discover that day that it is plenty hard. There was more to sailing than we knew. We got out to the middle of the lake and just sat there. There wasn't much wind, and we couldn't go anywhere. We had no idea how to manipulate the sails, so we just sat there for a long, long time. We finally got the attention of a man in a motorboat, and he towed us to shore. We returned the sailboat to the rental shop, feeling humiliated and defeated, and never tried sailing again. My advice to anyone who wants to sail is to take an experienced sailor with you.

I've come to see that experience as a metaphor of a journey with God. At some point in our lives, we decided to love and serve God. How hard can it be to sail through life with God? The answer, we eventually discover, is that it's plenty hard. At least occasionally, or even frequently, we find ourselves stranded at sea with no wind blowing. Where did God go? What happened to our passion? Where's the wind of the spirit? Who, or what, is available to rescue us?

Those were the questions the Ephesians were asking when John wrote 1 John to them. They were dealing with confusion and disillusionment, two conditions that made the spiritual wind stop blowing in their lives. When you're dealing with confusion and disillusionment, it's almost impossible to feel any wind at all.

So John wrote to them, trying to help them feel the wind. At least he could tell them how to operate the sails, how master sailors like himself had successfully navigated tricky spiritual waters. The first part of his letter dealt with the truth about loving God, and he offered them some practical things they needed to know and do to love God honestly and passionately. He told them to get focused, get real, get busy, and get eccentric, and then added one more piece of advice. In 3:1-10, he tells them to get challenged, to realize who they really are and to be challenged by their identity.

Who are they? What is their true identity? Here's how John answers those questions:

> See what love the Father has given us, that we should be called the children of God; and that is what we are. The reason the world does not know us is that it did not know him. Beloved, we are God's children now; what we will be has not yet been revealed. What we do know is this: when he is revealed, we will be like him, for we will see him as he is. And all who have this hope in him purify themselves, just as he is pure. (3:1-3)

Here's John's challenge in a nutshell: remember who you are, and live up to your identity.

Those Christians in Ephesus were ordinary people—farmers, fishermen, housewives, teenagers, and children. As Christians, they were probably looked upon as a bit strange and deluded by their unbelieving neighbors. They certainly didn't think of themselves as anything special. Quite to the contrary, they may have suffered from a collective inferiority complex.

But John begged to differ—and so did some of the other New Testament writers. Hear Peter in 1 Peter 2:9-10: "But you are a chosen race, a royal priesthood, a holy nation, God's own people, in order that you may proclaim the mighty acts of him who called you out of darkness into his marvelous light. Once you were not a people, but now you are God's people; once you had not received mercy, but now you have received mercy."

I once read a story about a young prince whose father, the king, pinned a purple ribbon on the boy's shirt to remind him that he was royalty. From time to time, the king would "appeal to the purple" to challenge the boy to live up to his royal identity. Peter and John did the same thing to those early Christians. They appealed to the purple by reminding their readers that they were children of God, sons and daughters of a King. They wanted those Christians to remember who they were and to live up to their identity as the children of God.

"Child of God": what a crucial reality to add to our "identity sack." We all carry with us each day an invisible "identity sack" that tells us who we are, or at least who we *think* we are. Who are we? Class clown. Star athlete. Ugly duckling. Inept bumbler. Compassionate rescuer. Guilty sinner. Embarrassed fool. And countless more. We carry these identities in our sack everywhere we go, and they determine how we play our role in the world. We each live out the identities we carry in our sack.

Here's one we dare not forget, according to John: child of God. That means we are created for a purpose, valued beyond measure, and the apple of God's eye. God feels about us the way we feel about our own precious sons and daughters—and would even die in our place if he had to. In fact, that's exactly what God did. Of all the identities we carry around with us, this one is the most important. If we know we are loved and valued by God, we will not only feel good about ourselves but will also be motivated to "live up to the purple," to live with dignity and grace to please the One who loves us so much. We will want to walk worthy of the One who pinned that ribbon on our shirts.

That means that we can't stay in the old system, what John calls "the world." If we are truly children of God, we become like God's son, Jesus, who committed no sin at all: "You know that he was revealed to take away sins, and in him there is no sin. No one who abides in him sins; no one who sins has either seen him or known him" (3:6). As royalty, we're expected to behave like royalty.

But wait a minute. There seems to be a major problem here. John has already told us in chapter 1 to get real and quit pretending to be holy and innocent. He has told us to be honest and admit that we have sinned so that we can bask in the incredible grace of God. How can John now tell us not to sin, that if we sin we're not really children of God? Which is it—confess our sin or try to be sinless?

In chapter 1, John is talking about "sins," those occasional lapses we all have when we stumble, fall short of God's will, and wander off the narrow road. When we do that, we are to admit our mistake and get back on the road that will take us to joy. But here, in chapter 3, John is talking about "sin," continually living in the world's domination system as if that's where we belong. He's talking about deliberately and consistently choosing the broad road as the road we plan to travel. No one who does that, he says, has a clue about really serving God: "Those who have been born of God do not sin, because God's seed abides in them; they cannot sin, because they have been born of God" (3:9).

William Barclay puts it this way:

> John is not setting before us a terrifying perfectionism; but he is demanding a life which is ever on the watch against sin, a life in which sin is not the normal accepted way but the abnormal moment of defeat. John is not saying that the person who abides in God cannot sin; but he is saying that the person who abides cannot continue to be a deliberate sinner.[8]

And why not choose to be a deliberate sinner? Because we are children of God. Because we dare not betray the One who loves us and sustains us. Because to sin deliberately is to take advantage of grace. Because to be less than we are causes God great pain.

When we think about Jesus' story of the prodigal son, we typically think of the pain of the son out there in the far country. He was miserable, ashamed, and lonely, yet all of his suffering was his own fault.

But what about the pain of the father? He was miserable, lonely, and worried sick about his son. Every day he stood on the front porch looking longingly down the road, hoping to catch a glimpse of his boy coming home. When he does see him coming, he runs down the road to greet him, gives him a bear hug, and welcomes him home with no strings attached. I would like to think that part of the motivation the son felt to go home was not just his own pain but his father's pain too. He couldn't bear to break his father's heart.

What John says in these verses is in that same spirit. We are children of God, beloved by a Father who wants only the best for us, who wants us to know the joy and security of being at home. As God's child, we cannot knowingly sin and disappoint him. We cannot bear the thought of breaking God's heart.

Being children of God not only gives us a healthy self-concept; it also gives us great motivation not to sin.

CONCLUSION

I can remember a time when there were three options on television—ABC, NBC, or CBS. Now my cable TV has so many stations I can't even tell you how many I receive. I know there are stations I have never watched. I can also remember a time when there were only three church options in the little town where I served as pastor. We had a Baptist church, a Presbyterian church, and a Lutheran church. Those who chose the Lutheran church had to drive into the country to get there. Now, when I drive through my current hometown of Austin, Texas, I can't tell you how many churches, mosques, fellowships, synagogues, and other places of worship I see. To say the world has changed in my lifetime is putting it mildly.

While that multiculturalism and multispiritualism have infused us with excitement and diversity, they have also increased our level of confusion. With all the options now available to us, who knows what to believe anymore? Who knows which option in the cafeteria of spiritual solutions is the best one? Who knows if there's even one truth that is truer than all the others?

Because we're living in such a confusing culture, the little book of 1 John is especially relevant to us. John was writing to people in a similar situation. They were dealing with conflicting doctrines about Christ, and they were also dealing with doubt and disillusionment in their own faith. They weren't sure who or what to believe anymore, and they were on the verge of drifting into spiritual "Never-Never Land."

John tried to nail down basic truths to give them some anchors. If they truly wanted to love God, they needed to

- *get focused on Christ.* They needed to quit bogging down in inconsequential issues and trivial pursuits and look long and hard at Jesus Christ.
- *get real about their sin.* They needed to quit trying to play games and impressing one another and be honest in confessing their humanity. They were sinners, and admitting that fact would enable them to be both honest and forgiven.

- *get busy doing the gospel.* They needed to move beyond thinking and feeling and start doing. The gospel was something to be lived in practical, tangible ways.
- *get eccentric by daring to be different from the people around them.* They had stepped out of one world and into another, and they needed to remember that.
- *get challenged by living up to their true identity.* They might have thought of themselves as farmers, fishermen, housewives, or students, but their primary identity was "child of God."

When John wanted to teach the early Christians the truth about loving God, those were the anchors he laid down for them. In our kind of exciting but confusing world, those anchors still give us some pillars on which to build a credible faith.

QUESTIONS FOR REFLECTION AND DISCUSSION

1. Which is our biggest threat today: (1) doctrinal heresy or (2) personal doubt and disillusionment?
2. When you get focused on Christ, what one facet of his life most inspires or challenges you?
3. Do you think we still play *charades* and *denial?* Do you think it is true that our society is hooked on image and advertising? Have we become a nation of victims?
4. Discuss the importance of knowing the truth, feeling the truth, and doing the truth. How do they affect each other? Which do you think is most important?
5. What does it mean to be a Christian eccentric? In what specific ways are Christians nonconformists? Who would you like to be famous to?
6. What does it mean to be a child of God? What does that biblical image imply about us?
7. What does our being children of God imply about God?
8. Are multiculturalism and multispiritualism a blessing or a curse? How can we best relate to people who do not share our beliefs about God?

SUGGESTIONS FOR WORSHIP AND PREACHING

An Order of Worship

This service focuses on 1 John 3:1-7 where John discusses what it means to be "children of God." That phrase not only defines our identity but also gives us some marching orders.

The Worship of God

"See what love the Father has given us, that we should be called the children of God" (1 John 3:1).

Spoken Call to Worship

The Chiming of the Hour

Hymn: "Give Thanks"

Invocation

Choral Meditation: "Find Us Faithful" (John Mohr, arranged by Tom Fettke, copyright 1988 by Birdwing Music/Jonathan Mark Music)

Hymn: "God of Grace and God of Glory"

Receiving Tithes and Offerings

Offertory Prayer

Word of the Lord: 1 John 3:1-7

    Worship Leader: This is the word of the Lord.

    Congregation: Thanks be to God.

Anthem: "Many Gifts, One Spirit" (Allen Pote, copyright 1986 by Coronet Press)

Sermon: "The Children of God"

Hymn of Response: "The Servant Song"

Choral Benediction: "With One Heart" (Mark Patterson, copyright 1998 by Choristers Guild)

Postlude

A Sermon Sketch: "The Children of God" (1 John 3:1-7)

Introduction

First John 3 begins with some amazingly good news: "See what love the Father has given us, that we should be called children of God; and that is what we are" (3:1a). What a great truth to celebrate! God has showered us with love and declared us to be his children.

But as we read further, we're reminded of some of those "good-news, bad-news" jokes we've heard ("The good news is that you get to play golf every day in heaven; the bad news is that your first tee time is eight o'clock tomorrow morning"). There must be a thousand jokes that follow that pattern.

The good news is that we are the children of God, but John has made a pledge to be honest with his readers, so he also tells us the "rest of the story."

The World Will Not Understand Us
The good news is that we are children of God: the bad news is that the world will not understand us. John makes it crystal clear in 1 John 2:15-17, and other places in his letter, that Christians are on a collision course with popular culture. Clarence Jordan once said that if we want to follow God, we need to find out where the world is heading and then go in the opposite direction. The children of God are destined for a life of nonconformity.

We Will Still Have Some Uncertainty
The good news is that we are children of God; the bad news is that we will still have some uncertainty. In verses 2-3, John says that we are the children of God now, but what happens to us in the future has not yet been revealed. What we do know, he says, is that we will be transformed into the image of Christ. But, as we know, Christ himself had to suffer and die. The children of God are not guaranteed an easy road or easy answers. As Paul put it, we're destined to see "through a glass darkly" (1 Cor 13:12). Being a child of God doesn't remove all mystery and uncertainty from our lives.

We Have to Do More than Talk
The good news is that we are children of God; the bad news is that we have to do more than talk about it. In verses 4-7, John spells out the responsibility for all who are children of God. The children of God live like their Father: "No one who sins has either seen him or known him" (2:6b). John wants us to *know* the truth and *feel* the truth, but mostly he wants us to *do* the truth.

Conclusion
The early church was made up of common people—farmers, fisherman, housewives, teenagers, and children. Some of them were even slaves. But the

New Testament writers worked hard at reminding those early Christians that they had a unique and special identity. As John reminds them in the first verse of 1 John, they were beloved children of God. Should they ever stumble into self-pity or should the world ever throw verbal stones at them, they shouldn't despair. They should just remember who they really are—children of God—and live with confidence and joy. But they should also know and accept the responsibility that comes with that title.

NOTES

1. Dallas Willard, *The Divine Conspiracy* (New York: HarperCollins, 1998) 94.

2. Ibid., 55.

3. Frederick Buechner, *Wishful Thinking* (New York: Harper & Row, 1973) 27.

4. Charles Sykes, *A Nation of Victims* (New York: St. Martin's Press, 1992) 11.

5. Ibid., 15.

6. William Barclay, *The Letters of John and Jude* (Louisville: Westminster John Knox Press, 1976) 42.

7. Naomi Nye, "Famous," in *Words under the Words: Selected Poems of Naomi Nye* (Portland OR: Far Corner Books, 1995) 13.

8. Barclay, *Letters of John and Jude*, 81.

THE TRUTH ABOUT LOVING PEOPLE

Focal Text—1 John 3:11–4:21

John saw much in the gnostic heresy that he thought needed to be challenged. As we discovered in session 1, Gnosticism's Christology implied some truths about God that John simply could not abide. If it was true, as the gnostics claimed, that Jesus wasn't a real human being with real flesh and blood, that meant that God couldn't identify with real human beings with real flesh and blood. God could remain a distant celestial being, untouched by temptation and suffering. And that is precisely how the gnostics viewed God. The gnostics' God was precise, perfect, and pain-free.

But John's God was different. John's God had become a man, faced temptation, experienced suffering and death, and come out victorious on the other side. John's God had endured all the ups and downs of normal human life and could readily relate to normal human beings. And John, and the other biblical writers, thought that was crucial. They believed that Jesus' incarnation was a pivotal part of his messiahship. So, John spent the first part of 1 John trying to get his Ephesian readers to know the truth about God. In 1 John 1:1–3:10, he not only took the gnostics to task but also put down some theological anchors he wanted his readers to embrace.

John also knew, though, that Gnosticism had implications for ministry and service, so he then turned his attention to the truth about loving people (3:11–4:21). Think about it: a person who believed the tenets of Gnosticism would place little emphasis on ministering to physical needs. The gnostics were focused on soul and spirit but not on anything physical or material. They would have been interested in an esoteric study of divine truth, for instance, but they would have had little interest in working in the soup kitchen. They would have enjoyed studying theology in the church library, but they would have had

Gnosticism

"Gnosticism" [from Greek *gnōsis*, knowledge] is a general term that describes a diverse religious movement sometimes associated with the rise of Christianity (although some scholars have theorized that Gnosticism has its roots in pre-Christian religions, instead of being merely an offshoot of Christianity). Its adherents are usually called "gnostics." Apparently Gnosticism drew its own theology from many different and varying sources. Thus certain, select aspects of both Judaism and Christianity may be found within its various expressions. Since, as their name implies, gnostics believed that they were privy to a secret knowledge about the divine, specific information about these sects is difficult to come by. In fact, the term "Gnosticism" is a very general, rather inclusive term used by scholars to refer to a number of groups that share certain similar beliefs in general but whose particular doctrinal emphases vary in specifics ways from group to group. In general, the term refers to those religious groups who differentiate the evil (material order) of this world (often identified with the God of the OT) from the good (spiritual order) of a higher, more abstract God revealed by Jesus Christ. Gnostics regard this world and all of its material order as evil and irredeemable. But they also believe in a hidden wisdom or knowledge available only to a select group as necessary for salvation or escape from this world. Certain sayings of Jesus were very appealing to the gnostics, and they apparently incorporated some of these into their belief systems, but only those that fit their suppositions.

The gnostics are alluded to in the Bible, for example, in 1 Timothy 1:4 and 1 Timothy 6:20, and possibly the entirety of Jude. These and other texts are sometimes lumped together and labeled "anti-gnostic references." Apparently some gnostics held that Christ was pure spirit and only "appeared" to have a physical body. Such a heretical view, from the orthodox point of view, might have been a contributing factor when the early Christians finally came to understand Jesus' nature as "fully God and fully man." Generally, the attitude among the early Christians was that Gnosticism was heretical and its adherents posed a grave danger to orthodoxy and should be disavowed and avoided.

Charles W. Hedrick, "Gnosticism," *Mercer Dictionary of the Bible* (ed. Watson E. Mills; Macon GA: Mercer University Press, 1990) 333–35.

no interest at all in building a house for the homeless. Their focus was on the *head*—not the *heart* and certainly not the *hands*.

John takes on the gnostics in verses like 3:17: "How does God's love abide in anyone who has the world's needs and sees a brother or sister in need and yet refuses to help?" That was a most un-gnostic kind of question, which is exactly why John posed it. He wanted his readers to know that following Jesus meant doing what Jesus did—feed the hungry, heal the sick, care for the physical needs of people. He wanted them to know that ministry and service were to be aimed at the whole person, at the body as well as the soul.

In this second session, we will examine the truth about loving people. John lays out three truths for us to ponder.

GET PERSONAL (3:11-24)

Two television commercials recently caught my attention. One was for a local television station, advertising its news, weather, and sports. The gist of the commercial was that our personal world is the most important one, that the world revolves around "me and mine," and that this station would tell "me and mine" all we need to know to stay informed.

The second commercial was for an oil company, and it began with the question, "Wouldn't it be great if the world revolved around you?" Then it went on to say that at their gas stations, that's exactly what happens. At their gas stations, the world revolves around you, and when you pull in all your needs are met.

Both of those commercial play to our self-interest. But honestly, don't we find their messages attractive? I tend to agree that the most important news in the world is whatever happens to me and mine. I also think it would be wonderful if the world did revolve around me. I probably remember those two commercials because I happen to agree with them. The people who wrote them tapped into a self-absorption that I, and I assume most people, have. I once heard a certain sports star described like this: "He's always seen the world as something that should adjust to him." Me, too, I'm afraid.

But we are also people of faith who have pledged our allegiance to Jesus Christ. Because of that, we know that we can't be completely self-absorbed and be true to our marching orders. If we occasionally forget those marching orders, a letter like 1 John is quick to remind us what they are. This particular passage in 1 John 3 is so persistent, we can scarcely *not* hear its message. It's almost as if John thinks we might be hard of hearing, so he shouts his message loud and long:

- "For this is the message which you have heard from the beginning, that we should love one another." (3:11)
- "We know that we have passed from life unto death because we love one another." (3:14)
- ". . . we ought to lay down our lives for one another." (3:16b)
- "Little children, let us love, not in word or speech, but in truth and action." (3:18)

• "And this is his commandment, that we should believe in the name of his Son Jesus Christ and love one another, just as he commanded us." (3:24)

By the time we get to the end of these verses, we're saying, "Okay, John. We get it. We're not supposed to be self-absorbed. We're supposed to find someone to love in a tangible way. In fact, we can't even claim to love God if we can't love people."

Of course, John wasn't the first one to say this. Jesus not only said it but also lived it in a radical way. When we think about Jesus' strategy for living and for building his kingdom, we realize how simple that strategy was. Jesus never held any political office, received any impressive titles, wrote any book, built any building, or sought any fame. He never passed any legislation or assembled any army of crusaders. What he did was so simple it changed the world: he loved a few people in tangible, specific ways.

He basically gave himself to twelve people . . . because that was the only way to change the whole world. When he died, he left behind no buildings, books, money, or credentials. He left behind a handful of people he had loved *personally*. It is telling that John referred to himself as "the one Jesus loved."

In this part of 1 John, he reminds his readers to love that way, too. Jesus had loved him in a way that changed his life forever. Now, John wanted to love others that way, and he wanted his readers to love others that way as well. That, in fact, is the very heart of our gospel, the very rhythm that is supposed to be throbbing in our lives: we receive the love of God, and then we give it away to the people around us.

When my kids were young, I would occasionally help them with their homework. Sometimes I would help them reduce fractions. We would take a bunch of complicated, cumbersome numbers and reduce them to their simplest form. That's not a bad thing to do in our theology either—take all the complicated, cumbersome stories and doctrines in the Bible and reduce them to their essence.

Fortunately, Jesus has done it for us. When a teacher of the law came to him and asked him to pinpoint the greatest commandment in all of the law, he was asking him to reduce spirituality to its indispensable core. It was a complicated, cumbersome thing that leader was asking Jesus to do because there were hundreds of commandments in the Old Testament. But Jesus was up to the task:

He said to him, "You shall love the Lord your God with all your heart, and with all your soul, and with all your mind." This is the greatest and first commandment. And the second is like it: "You shall love your neighbor as yourself." On these two commandments hang all the law and prophets. (Matt 22:37-40)

Reduce those thousands of words in the law to their essence and you come up with this: love God and love people. Everything in the law revolves around these two truths. If we're sometimes perplexed by the strangeness of Scripture and befuddled by some of the bizarre things we read there, it's nice to know that what it means is *love God and love people.*

In these verses, John's emphasis on the second of those two commandments is one most of us have known all our lives. We all know we're supposed to love others. "What the world needs now is love, sweet love, that's the only thing that there's just too little of." Even secular pop singers know that. So, the question then becomes, why don't we do a better job of it? If we know we're supposed to love people, why don't we do it? The answer, I think, is twofold.

First, *we forget.* We get careless and forget how indispensable our love is to our husband or wife, our kids or grandkids, our parents, our friends at church. We forget that every person we know has an invisible love tank that must be filled on a regular basis, and if it doesn't, that person will experience some kind of sickness. We forget that our calling as followers of Jesus is to fill those people's love tanks.

Second, *we get busy.* The kind of personal love John has in mind takes time. It's a personal and concentrated love. It can't be squeezed in around a bunch of other activities and priorities. If we take this part of 1 John seriously, we might have to step off the ladder of success and be a little less available to the world so that we can focus our attention on a few people. Personal love—Jesus' kind of love—is narrow, focused, tangible, and time-consuming.

Paula D'Arcy, in *Where the Wind Begins,* has written,

The formula for finding your own, primary mission is here: Put down this book. Walk outside your house, trailer, or apartment. Look in through a window. Now you see where Christ has sent you. Serving starts where you are. If you understand that your mission to the faces at your table, no matter how few, ranks in importance with the mission of a great evangelist to crowds of thousands, then you have begun to understand Love.[1]

When John encourages us to love in truth and action, this is what he has in mind. He's calling us to do something tangible for someone specific. In his book *Reawakenings*, Thomas Keating echoes this part of 1 John when he writes,

> When Mother Teresa picked up a dying man in the streets of Calcutta, she captured the imagination of the world. It was a striking symbol of God's concern for the poor. Each of us is surrounded by opportunities. We don't have to be invited to the United Nations or go to a summit conference to save the world. Divine love suggests a first step that needs to be taken here and now.[2]

"A first step that needs to be taken here and now." That's very much in the spirit of these verses.

Hugh Prather, in *Notes to Myself*, wrote,

> If only I had forgotten future greatness and looked at green things and the buildings and reached out to those around me and smelled the air. And ignored the expectations and self-styled obligations, and heard the rain on my roof, and put my arms around my wife. And it's not too late.[3]

The good news is that it's not too late. But the time to get personal is now.

GET SMART (4:1-6)

At the beginning of chapter 4, John abruptly shifts gears. He has been writing about the importance of loving the people around us, of getting personal the way Jesus did. Like Jesus, we are to love in action and truth. Love is not just something we say or feel; it is also something we do.

Then, suddenly, John moves in a new direction: "Beloved, do not believe every spirit, but test the spirits to see whether they are from God; for many false prophets have gone out into the world" (4:1). He is referring again to the gnostics, who were leading Christians away from the truth about Christ, so he adds this explanatory note: "By this you know the spirit of God: every spirit that confesses that Jesus Christ has come in the flesh is from God, and every spirit that does not confess Jesus is not from God" (4:2-3a).

These verses introduce us to a second idea in our quest to learn the truth about loving people. While we are to get personal and love people in the specific, tangible way that Jesus loved people, we are also to get smart and not believe everything people tell us or try to get us to believe. We are to be as innocent as doves . . . and also as wise as serpents.

Our best example, as always, is Jesus, who loved people unreservedly while also rejecting the legalistic religion of the scribes and Pharisees and even rejecting the alluring suggestions of his own disciples to forsake the cross. Jesus was personal enough to love people in specific, tangible ways and smart enough to reject the people who wanted him to embrace a lie. His love was both personal and smart.

Discerning the truth in our day—or any day—is not easy. We live in a time when all of us are confronted by too much information, what is often dubbed "information overload." Consider, as one example, the information we have available to us about taking care of our hearts. If we want to prevent coronary disease and live long, healthy lives, what do we need to do to protect our hearts?

I once saw a list of seventy ingestible substances that had been tested to determine their effect on a person's heart. The list included guavas, almonds, walnuts, apples, onions, black tea, simple and complex carbohydrates, corn oil, olive oil, alcohol, garlic, coffee, caffeine, magnesium, potassium, and calcium. Studies have also been done that related heart health to body shape, height, baldness, pets, snoring, menopause, music, and sex. No one can possibly absorb all the data, and information overload causes us to throw up our hands and quit trying.

What is true of heart health is also true for just about any other topic we want to study. Which school of psychological thought should we believe? Which car should we drive? Which diet should we try? Which religion should we believe? Which church should we attend? The number of questions is almost endless and so are the answers to those questions. We're like people in a cafeteria line, staring at so many entrees that we don't know what to eat. We have so many options we may starve to death.

John's readers at the end of the first century didn't have all the information we have today, but they had enough to make life confusing. That's why John tells them to test the spirits to see which are from God. There were many different spirits vying for their allegiance. And the plumb line he uses to determine which spirit is from God is this: does it match up with who Jesus was and what Jesus did? As I said, he had the gnostics in mind when he wrote this, but this question is a helpful tool in any generation. When we try to make hard decisions, it is wise to ask, does this match up with the spirit and wisdom of Christ? Does this sound like something Jesus would do?

John, as he often does in 1 John, draws a sharp distinction in these verses. Christ or antichrist? God or world? Spirit of truth or spirit of error? As Jesus did before him, he pictures life as a matter of choosing which road we will travel. He reminds us that life is filled with crossroads and that we keep having to choose which road we will travel. He also reminds us that the quality of our lives will be determined by the choices we make at those crossroads.

The old biblical word for this choosing of a road or path is "repentance." It is a word in serious need of a PR campaign. Let the pastor announce a sermon on repentance and people will stay away in droves. Repentance conjures up notions of a red-faced preacher screaming words of condemnation to cowering sinners. No one thinks of repentance as something positive, but it is. Repentance means we can change our minds, change our lives, and move in a completely new direction. Repentance means we can get off the old road that has been taking us to misery and get on a new road that will take us to joy. In John's terms, we can choose Christ over antichrist, God over world, and truth over error.

Not surprisingly, the people who are the best candidates for repentance are the people who are disillusioned with the way things are. The person most likely to choose the narrow road is the one disgusted with life on the broad road. Whenever we question the conventional wisdom of the world—how to be happy, what is important, how to have good relationships, the purpose of our existence, how to spend money, how to make a living—we're prime candidates for repentance.

John wanted the Ephesian Christians to look at the two roads before them and choose the way of Christ. He knew it was the road of victory: "the one who is in you is greater than the one who is in the world" (1:4b). But he also knew that saying yes to Christ meant saying no to the world. Choosing one road always means getting off another road. Leo Tolstoy, the Russian novelist, once wrote that if we will accept the clear and simple teaching of Christ, we will see that we live in a world of big lies.

In *A Long Obedience in the Same Direction*, Eugene Peterson has a prayer that is very much in the spirit of this passage in 1 John:

Rescue me from the lies of advertisers who claim to know what I need and what I desire, from the lies of entertainers who promise a cheap way to joy, from the lies of politicians who pretend to instruct me in power and morality, from the lies of psychologists who offer to shape my behavior and my morals so that I will live long, happily, and successfully, from the lies of religionists who "heal the wounds of this people lightly," from the lies of moralists who pretend to promote me to the office of captain of my fate, from the lies of pastors who "leave the commandment of God, and hold fast the tradition of men" (Mk 7:8). Rescue me from the person who tells me of life and omits Christ, who is wise in the ways of the world and ignores the movement of the Spirit.[4]

This moving from a world of lies to the truth of God is supposed to be a constant process. If we're smart, repentance happens all the time. Our blood pressure gets too high, so we repent. Our kids start growing distant and surly, so we repent. Our spirits start to sag and we grow lethargic, so we repent. God starts to seem distant and unreal, so we repent. If we're smart, we take constant readings of our physical, emotional, spiritual, and relational health, and then we make the necessary changes to get on the road of wholeness.

The Hopi Indians had a fine word for which we have no English equivalent. They spoke of "koyaanisqatsi," which basically meant "life out of balance." They believed that life was supposed to be lived with a certain harmony and symmetry, what we might call "in the flow." But when a person's life gets out of balance, that person has the dreaded condition of "koyaanisqatsi" and needs to recognize and correct it.

We have dozens of words to describe what those Hopi Indians captured in one word: burnout, anxiety, stress, unfulfillment, fatigue, boredom. But the root problem is that our lives are out of balance and need to be put back in line. To use John's terminology, we need to turn our backs on the spirit of error and start living in the spirit of truth.

When John wanted to help the Ephesian Christians come alive spiritually and when he wanted them to know the truth about loving people, he said to them, "Get smart. Be discerning. Not everything out there in the world is for you. And not everyone you know is a

Listen to What God Says to the Believer

1. You are forgiven (1:9)
2. You know God (2:4-6)
3. You know and belong to the truth (2:20-21; 3:19)
4. You are the children of God (3:1-2, 10)
5. You are loved (4:10-11)

Thomas F. Johnson, *1, 2, and 3 John*, NIBCNT (Peabody MA: Hendrickson, 1993), 99.

trustworthy guide. So test the spirits. Use Jesus Christ as your measuring rod, and believe and do those things that are in harmony with him."

It was true for the Christians in Ephesus, and it is still true for us. When it comes to loving people, we need to get personal. But we also need to get smart.

GET MOTIVATED (4:7-21)

In 2000, Malcolm Gladwell wrote a fascinating bestseller titled *The Tipping Point*.[5] The subtitle of the book is "How Little Things Make a Big Difference." The book is a compilation of times in history when little things made a big difference.

Gladwell mentions a little-watched television program on PBS called *Sesame Street*. The show was mired in low ratings and about to go under until the producers added a goofy character they called Big Bird. With the addition of Big Bird, the show took off and became a social phenomenon watched by millions of children. Big Bird was the surprising tipping point that turned the show around.

He also mentions "the broken windows theory" in New York City. The police in New York City started to tackle crime in a most unusual way. They started fixing broken windows throughout the city and removing graffiti from city walls. When they did, an amazing thing happened: the crime rate plummeted. It turns out that broken windows and graffiti invited anarchy, and their removal sparked a remarkable turnaround in the city.

I mention Gladwell's book because our next verses in 1 John contain a tipping point, one of those little things that makes a big difference. Tucked away in 1 John 4 is a little verse that, once we understand it, changes everything in our relationship with God—and in our motivation to love other people. It becomes, or can become, a tipping point that puts the Christian life in a new light.

The tipping point is one simple sentence: "We love because he first loved us" (4:19). That one verse sums up the central truth John wants to convey in 1 John 4:7-21. God loved us *first*. Before we ever uttered a prayer, attended a worship service, read the Bible, went on a mission trip, or built a house for Habitat, God loved us unreservedly: "In this is love, not that we loved God but that he loved us and sent his Son to be the atoning sacrifice for our sins" (4:10).

God's love comes first, and everything in the Christian's life is a response to that incredible love.

But it's all too easy to forget that. It's all too easy to fall into the trap of believing that we coax God into loving us by doing good things. If we can just pray enough, give enough, worship enough, serve enough, and witness enough, God will notice our impressive devotion and reward us with his love. We can begin to think that our love for God is the engine that drives the train of Christian discipleship.

But John says no. God's love for us is the engine that drives the train of Christian discipleship. I once knew a youth speaker who would address youth groups in conferences and retreats. He would begin one

> **Personal Implication of "God Is Love"**
>
> When in fact we take the metaphor "God is love" and as in I John 4 we understand it personally: He is the One who loves. This personal way in which Scripture speaks is not in any way childish or naïve or anthropomorphic . . . . The personal way in which Holy Scripture speaks corresponds absolutely and exclusively to the fact that God is not something, but someone, the One from whom man merely holds in fee the possibility of being one himself.
>
> Karl Barth, *Church Dogmatics* 2/1 (1957): 286.

session by asking the youth, "What do you have to do to get God to love you?" The answers were not surprising: Go to church. Help others. Pray. Read the Bible. Obey your parents. And so forth.

Then the speaker would tell the youth that their answers were all incorrect. He would tell them that the correct answer to the question is "Nothing." You have to do absolutely nothing to get God to love you. God's love is a gift, and all of those things the youth mentioned are to be done not to earn God's love but to express gratitude that they already have it.

Even if we learned that truth as youth, it is easy to forget it as adults. Everything in our culture is built on works, and John's message of amazing grace and the unmerited love of God is decidedly countercultural. Like the Galatian Christians, we tend to fall away from grace and to fall back into the comfortable clutches of legalism.

But if we can remember 1 John 4:19—"We love because he first loved us"—that verse is a tipping point that changes everything:

• Church becomes a community of celebration, a place where we neither harangue people nor try to whip them into shape, but where we teach and live the good news that we are all loved beyond measure.

- Prayer becomes not so much asking God for things as thanking God for the blessings and love we don't deserve but receive all the time.
- Evangelism becomes not so much presenting propositions for people to accept as inviting people to a party and daring them to believe the news of God's unbelievable love.
- Discipleship becomes not trying to win brownie points from God by doing good things but living in gratitude that we are held, embraced, and fortified by a love that will not let us go.
- Personal relationships become not competitive sparring sessions to see who can be the most powerful and successful but occasions for sharing the grace we have received from God with another person.

This last consequence of the 1 John 4:19 tipping point is the one John stresses most here. He has already mentioned that loving people involves getting personal and getting smart, but here he says it also involves getting motivated. The incredible love that God has for us is to motivate us to love others the same way: "Beloved, since God loved us so much, we also ought to love one another" (4:11). Then he hits the note he sounds several times in this letter: "The commandment we have from him is this: those who love God must love their brothers and sisters also" (4:21). And, we might add, with the same kind of gracious love God has given us.

Once we understand the truth John is describing in 1 John 4:7-21, everything changes. It's just a slight tweaking of our old understanding of things, but what a difference it makes. It's a tipping point that ends up changing our understanding of church, prayer, evangelism, discipleship, relationships, and more. It's a tipping point that sets us on a whole new journey with God.

In 1996, a part-time actress and playwright by the name of Rebecca Wells published *Divine Secrets of the Ya-Ya Sisterhood.* Its arrival in bookstores was not a major event. When Wells gave a reading at a bookstore in Greenwich, Connecticut, seven people showed up. The book got a smattering of reviews and sold 15,000 copies in hardback.

A year later, *Divine Secrets of the Ya-Ya Sisterhood* came out in paperback. The first edition of 18,000 copies sold out in a few months, exceeding expectations. Then the paperback sales reached 30,000, and everyone was surprised. Wells and her publisher soon realized that something wonderful had happened: women's book clubs in northern California had discovered the book, and these book clubs were telling other book clubs about it. Those book clubs became the book's tipping point, and, last I heard, the book has been through 48 printings and sold 2.5 million copies.

As amazing as stories like that are, they all pale beside what happens to individuals and churches when they realize the truth of this passage in 1 John 4. This "little truth" about God's love coming first, about a love that arrives with no strings attached, sets people free. It makes tired Christians glad and sad churches happy. It unleashes personal renewal and church revival.

And it's all because of one little truth: we love because he first loved us.

The Love of God for Us

1. Its source: God, who is actually love (4:8, 16)
2. Its very character: outgoing in sending and giving (4:10)
3. Its activity: self-giving for the sake of the other (3:16)
4. Its effect: expiation for our sins (4:10), that we may live through him (4:9), the salvation of the world (4:14)

John Painter, *1, 2, and 3 John* (SP; ed. Daniel J. Harrington, S.J.; (Collegeville MN: Liturgical Press, 2002), 276–77.

CONCLUSION

I am a confessed bookaholic and have bought thousands of books in my life. I don't even want to know how much money I have invested in my personal library. I am always happiest when I am under the spell of a good book because it gives me something to look forward to. Is there anything better than nestling into bed early with a novel that transports you to a new world or a nonfiction book that challenges you with new truth? Conversely, is there anything worse than being bookless?

As I peruse my shelves, I realize that my books fall into three primary categories. I have fiction books, theology books, and psychology/relationship books. Some of my books entertain me with a good story. Some of my books instruct me about God. And some of my books instruct me about people. I suppose the books I have bought over the years say something significant about my life. I want to be entertained. I want to connect with God. And I want to connect with people. And I suspect those desires are not unique to me.

John directly speaks to two of those quests in 1 John. He speaks to the truth about God in 1 John 1:1–3:10, and he speaks to the truth about people in 1 John 3:11–4:21. His counsel to the Ephesian Christians at the end of the first century filters down to us today and still offers us three truths to ponder when we think about loving people:

• *When it comes to loving people, we are to get personal.* We are to love in action and in truth the way Christ did. Our love of others is to be specific, tangible, and focused.

• *When it comes to loving people, we are to get smart.* Loving people doesn't mean we have to accept every idea or truth people propose to us. We must "test the spirits" and measure all truth by the plumb line of Jesus Christ.

• *When it comes to loving people, we are to get motivated.* Our motivation comes from the love of God, which has arrived in our lives with no strings attached. We love others because God first loved us.

> **Mainsprings to Loving**
>
> 1. The nature of God as love (4:8, 16)
> 2. The command to love one another (4:7, 12)
> 3. The act of God in loving us (4:9-10)
> 4. The appeal of completing the love of God (4:12)

I suppose we could sum up John's truth about loving people by saying our relationships are to be marked by focused love, discerning wisdom, and unusual grace. If we can relate to people like that, "God lives in us, and his love is perfected in us" (4:12). We're learning to love the way Jesus loved.

QUESTIONS FOR REFLECTION AND DISCUSSION

1. If gnostic thinking had carried the day, how would that have changed the Christian movement? What would that have done to the ministry and focus of the church?

2. Which is our biggest enemy in loving the people around us—forgetfulness or busyness? Who are the specific people in your "parish," the people you are called to love in specific and tangible ways?

3. How can we be as innocent as doves and also as wise as serpents? Do you ever feel overwhelmed by information overload? What are some of the big lies propagated by our culture?

4. Do you agree that 1 John 4:19 is a key tipping point in Scripture? How did the truth of that verse become real in your own life?

5. How can we keep the commandment to love others from becoming "old hat" to us? How can we love people who are sometimes very unlovable?

SUGGESTIONS FOR WORSHIP AND PREACHING

An Order of Worship

This service focuses on 1 John 4:19 where John writes about God loving us *first*. This passage can be a "tipping point" in the lives of people who are schooled in working to earn God's approval. The following service can enable all of us to remember how good our good news really is. It can also give us needed motivation to love others.

The Worship of God
"We love because he first loved us." (1 John 4:19)
Spoken Call to Worship
The Chiming of the Hour
Processional Hymn: "Joyful, Joyful, We Adore Thee"
Children's Sermon
Choral Meditation: "Here I Am" (Words: Tom Long and Allen Pote, Music: Allen Pote, arranged by Tom Schrader, copyright 1996 by Hope Publishing Co.)
Prayer
Hymn: "Pass It On"
Receiving of Tithes and Offerings
The Singing of the Doxology
The Offertory Prayer
The Word of the Lord: 1 John 4:7-21
　　Worship Leader: This is the word of the Lord.
　　Congregation: Thanks be to God.
Choral Reflection: "Prayer of St. Francis" (Allen Pote, copyright 1986 by Hinshaw Music)
Sermon: "The Tipping Point"
Hymn of Response: "Grace Greater than Our Sin"
Spoken Benediction

Leader: Loving God, we thank you for loving us first.

Congregation: Now show us tangible ways to give that love to the people around us.

All: In the name and spirit of Christ we pray, Amen.

Postlude

A Sermon Sketch: "The Tipping Point" (1 John 4:19)

Introduction

Several years ago, Malcolm Gladwell wrote a bestselling book titled *The Tipping Point*. In the book, he gives example after example of little things that made a big difference. Seemingly insignificant actions ended up being tipping points that changed everything. Our verse this morning from 1 John is a biblical tipping point. It's just one little verse, but it can end up changing everything about our faith in God.

Trading Stamp Religion

Most religion today is built around works. It's what we could call "trading stamp religion." Some of you might be old enough to know what trading stamps are. If not, let me tell you that once upon a time, grocery stores gave shoppers trading stamps when they bought their groceries. You pasted your stamps in a book, and when you got enough you could trade them in for something you wanted—a lamp, or a mixer, or a flashlight.

Religion tends to work the same way. In any religious system, people save up their good works and hope to cash them in someday at the heavenly redemption center. If we have enough stamps in our book, God will reward us with eternal life. If our book happens to be mostly empty, God will frown upon us—and perhaps turn us away.

Making the Good News Good Again

In reality, though, Christianity is not a religion at all; it's the announcement of the *end* of religion. And that's where 1 John 4:19 comes in. It tells us that God loved us *first*. Before we ever said a prayer, gave a tithe, attended a worship service, read the Bible, or did one act of kindness, God already loved us. In other words, God loved us before we ever put one stamp in our book.

The one person in the Bible who most celebrates the end of "trading stamp religion" is the apostle Paul. He had grown up in a very religious system where he needed to obey laws, perform rituals, give offerings, and generally collect enough stamps to impress God with his goodness. Then he met Christ, learned that God loved him just as he was, and became the great ambassador of grace. Once he learned the truth that John declares in 1 John 4:19, his life was changed forever. He dropped religion of works and embraced the gospel of grace.

All Things New
The reason this one little truth is actually a very big truth is that it does change everything in our relationship with God. We move from obligation to celebration. Activities that once seemed to be heavy duties—going to church, praying, witnessing to our friends, reading the Bible, tithing, and so forth—are transformed into ways to thank God for his love. We no longer have to impress God with our goodness; instead we are impressed with the incredible goodness of God. And this incredible goodness of God gives us the motivation we need to love others. Freely we have received, and freely we give.

Conclusion
When you read Gladwell's book, you're amazed at the difference little things have made. Who would have thought that a goofy character named Big Bird would rescue a floundering kid's show named *Sesame Street* and turn it into a social phenomenon? Who knew that fixing broken windows and removing graffiti from the walls in New York City would greatly reduce the crime rate there?

And who knew that one little verse in 1 John 4 could transform everything about our relationship to God?

NOTES

1. Paula D'Arcy, *Where the Wind Begins* (Wheaton: Harold Shaw Publishers, 1984) 35.

2. Thomas Keating, *Reawakenings* (New York: Crossroad, 1992) 17.

3. Hugh Prather, *Notes to Myself* (New York: Bantam, 1993) 74.

4. Eugene Peterson, *A Long Obedience in the Same Direction* (Downers Grove IL: InterVarsity Press, 1980) 23.

5. Malcolm Gladwell, *The Tipping Point: How Little Things Make a Big Difference* (Little, Brown and Company, 2000.)

Session 3

THE TRUTH ABOUT THE DIFFERENCE JESUS MAKES

Focal Text—1 John 5:1-21

Since the gnostics were questioning key truths about Christ—and creating controversy and contention in the process—it is not surprising that John ends 1 John with a resounding affirmation of who Jesus was and what he did. In particular, John concludes his letter by telling his readers the truth about the difference Jesus makes in a person's life. And he does so with both confidence and certainty. There is nothing wishy-washy about John or his theology about Jesus. In the brief letter of 1 John, he uses the word "know" thirty-nine times, and he uses it eight times in this last chapter:

- "By this we know that we love the children of God, when we love God and obey his commandments." (5:2)
- "I write these things to you who believe in the name of the Son of God, so that you may know that you have eternal life." (5:13)
- "And if we know that he hears us in whatever we ask, we know that we have obtained the requests made of him." (5:15)
- "We know that those who are born of God do not sin . . . ." (5:18)
- "We know that we are God's children . . . ." (5:19)
- "And we know that the Son of God has come and has given us understanding so that we may know him who is true . . . ." (5:20)

In our culture, where everything once nailed down seems to be coming loose, John's insistence on knowing the truth may seem both dogmatic and arrogant. The cover of an *Utne Reader* several years ago captured the mood of our culture perfectly. Under the heading "Designer God," it showed a young boy with outstretched hands. He was wearing a yarmulke and locks of a Hasidic Jew, a Buddhist monk's robe, and a Christian cross. If you looked at him closely, you could also see two necklaces around his neck—one a ying-yang symbol of Taoism and the other a star and crescent from Islam. The subtitle on the cover asked, "In a mix-and-match world, why not create your own religion?"

The assumption behind that question is that we all have to create our own belief system, cobble together a mix-and-match religion that works for us, and then try to navigate our way through a treacherous culture. What works for you may not work for me and vice versa. We each have to find the truth that is true for us.

In that kind of world, John's thirty-nine "knows" sound strange and outdated. He actually thought he had the truth? He actually believed that Christ was the answer to people's problems? He actually believed that his truth was true for all people? He actually thought it was futile to cobble together one's own religion when God had done something so remarkable in Christ? Frankly, John may not be popular in our mix-and-match world where people just want to dabble. He *knew*, and he was not shy about saying so.

One thing John knew for certain was that Christ made a radical difference in a person's life. He knew that was true because his own life had been changed forever when he met Jesus. As he said in the opening words of his letter, "We declare to you what was from the beginning, what we have heard, what we have seen with our eyes, what we have looked at and touched with our hands, concerning the word of life—this life was revealed, and we have seen it and testify to it . . ." (1:1-2a).

The final chapter of 1 John is, no doubt, John's testimony. He is writing about his own experience and describing the difference Jesus has made in his life. And he knows that if Jesus could change his life so dramatically, he can do the same for others. He mentions four ways Jesus has transformed his life, four crucial ways Jesus makes a difference in the lives of the people who know and love him.

THE REASON FOR OUR VICTORY (5:1-5)

Three times in these verses John uses an arresting phrase—"conquer the world." He writes,

- ". . . whatever is born of God conquers the world." (5:4a)
- "And this is the victory that conquers the world, our faith." (5:4b)
- "Who is it that conquers the world but the one who believes that Jesus is the Son of God?" (5:5)

Make no mistake, though: the world can also conquer us. We can get steam-rolled by sin, confusion, stress, anger, and a host of other worldly enemies and end up lifeless and depressed. In the ongoing battle between human beings and the world, the world usually comes out on top. We can all think of people we know who have been pummeled by the world. Even more to the point, we can all think of times in our lives when the world has pummeled us, too.

John's phrase is arresting precisely because we need it so much. We need to know how to conquer the world and not let the world conquer us. He says, "And this is the victory that conquers the world, our faith" (5:4b), and proceeds in these verses to describe two facets of this faith that can conquer the world.

First, *it is a faith that focuses on loving people.* "Everyone who believes that Jesus is the Christ has been born of God, and everyone who loves the parent loves the child. By this we know that we love the children of God, when we love God and obey his commandments" (5:1-2). If we love God, the parent, we will also love people, the children of God. Loving God means loving people. It is a truth John has stressed so much in 1 John that we might wonder why he would address it again. And the answer must be because it was so needed among the Ephesian Christians at the end of the first century. There must have been Christians in that day who professed Christ and also ignored or despised people.

The world would be much easier to understand if Christians were always the people who are loving, gracious, kind, and long suffering. It would be easier

Conquering: A Presiding Metaphor in Revelation

The book of Revelation, belonging to the Johannine circle but at some remove, develops the motif of conquering while addressing believers under duress. Note the prominence of conquering in the letters to the seven churches in its first movement (1:7; 2:11, 17, 26; 3:5, 12, 21). The author offers conquering as a meaningful self-understanding of the Christian life. The theme affirms the divine victory over evil. "It is grounded in the almighty God who made this universe, and whose will cannot be finally frustrated by any power in heaven or earth or hell," wrote Beasley-Murray. "It is grounded in the God who has wrought redemption in and through Christ, the power of which is experienced in the world now, and the end of which is the subjection of all things to God."

G. R. Beasley-Murray, *Revelation* (London: Oliphants, 1974), 46.

if non-Christians were always the people who are mean, selfish, cruel, and petulant. We would know the Christians by their love, and we would know the non-Christians by their lack of love. It would be simple to discern the good guys from the bad guys in that kind of world, and the goal of the Christians would be to convert the non-Christians.

But honesty and accuracy demand that we confess that this is not the case. Sometimes Christians are mean, selfish, cruel, and petulant, and non-Christians are loving, gracious, kind, and long suffering. Sometimes Christians fall far short of the example of Jesus and need to look again at his life—or read again the letter of 1 John—and start loving both the Parent and his children.

John has made it clear throughout this letter that the only faith that can conquer the world, the only faith that can sustain us emotionally and spiritually and transform the people around us, is a faith that loves others. Our assignment is not to judge people, straighten people out, teach people, or even convert people; our assignment is to love people. We each have been given a parish to tend—a family, an office, a classroom, a Sunday school class, a ball team—and our ministry is to love the people in that parish. According to John, being faithful in loving those people will not only help them but will also give us a faith that conquers the world.

Second, *it is a faith that is not burdensome.* "For the love of God is this, that we obey his commandments. And his commandments are not burdensome, for whatever is born of God overcomes the world" (5:3-4a). Contrary to popular belief, the commandments of God don't burden us down with a bunch of "oughts" and "shoulds"; they liberate us to live with joy.

It is a sad thing that the world sees God as the Celestial Killjoy, intent on loading us down with religious ceremonies and laws that are destined to produce misery. The reason the world sees God this way is that so many Christians *are* loaded down with religious ceremonies and laws and seem miserable. The world looks at burdened, joyless Christians and assumes that is what Christianity does to people and what following God does to people. They think that God burdens people down with religious rules so they won't have the time or energy to kick up their heels and commit sin.

But John says the kind of faith that conquers the world is not burdensome. He has already described this kind of faith in chapter 4: "There is no fear in love, but perfect love casts out fear; for fear has to do with punishment, and whoever fears has not reached perfection in love. We love because he first loved us" (4:18-19). As we saw in the last session, all that we do in the Christian life—all of our praying, giving, preaching, teaching, serving, worshiping, and so forth—is done not to earn God's love but because we already have God's love. The burden to impress God is gone, replaced by the freedom to serve God out of gratitude.

No one in the Bible learned that lesson more clearly or proclaimed it more passionately than the apostle Paul. His old religion as a Pharisee was burdensome, loaded with laws, rituals, and expectations. When he met Christ, he got John's brand of religion: a gospel of grace that removed those misery-producing burdens. In *Traveling Light*, Eugene Peterson wrote,

> It was as if God said, "Listen, Paul, you have it all wrong. You have good
> ideas, your theology is intelligent enough, your sincerity is above reproach, but
> you have it all wrong. You think religion is a matter of knowing things and
> doing things. It is not. It is a matter of letting God do something for you—
> letting him love you, letting him save you, letting him bless you, letting him
> command you. Your part is to look and believe, to pray and obey."[1]

God says something like that to all of us. God wants to move us from burdensome religion to liberating gospel, but we have a hard time hearing that message. When we spend our whole lives earning our success—in school, sports, work, and even personal relationships—the message of grace that "we love because he first loved us" is not easy to comprehend. We feel more comfortable climbing the ladder of success than accepting a gift that arrives through no effort of our own.

So, according to John, those two facets of faith—loving others and dropping burdensome religion—can help us conquer the world. If we told John we had faith in Christ, he would likely ask us two pointed questions: "Is it a faith that loves people? Is it a faith that is liberating and joyful?" If we were to answer "yes," he would likely say we have a victorious faith that can conquer the world.

In his commentary on this passage, William Barclay writes,

> We have the indestructible hope of final victory. The world did its worst to
> Jesus. It hounded him and slandered him. It branded him heretic and friend
> of sinners. It judged him and crucified him and buried him. It did everything
> humanly possible to eliminate him—*and it failed.* After the cross came the
> resurrection; after the shame came the glory.[2]

When I was in college, our football team was something less than successful. No, let's tell it like it was: our team was terrible. We won five games in my four years of college. But things got a little better after I graduated, and once we pulled the upset of the year and beat our archrival. It was a huge and surprising upset, and, to celebrate the victory, the school left the scoreboard on all night. Reportedly, fans drove by throughout the night to gaze at the scoreboard and see the remarkable story it told: we won!

A lot of good things happen when we Christians go to church on Sunday. We get to study Scripture, hear good music, listen to an inspiring sermon, be with our church friends, and make important personal decisions. But we also get to see the scoreboard and remember our remarkable news: we won! Because of Christ, we won the war over evil and death. To put it in John's memorable phrase, we get to celebrate the fact that we've "conquered the world."

THE SOURCE OF OUR LIFE (5:6-12)

One thing that makes interpreting the Bible difficult is that we often are privy only to one side of a conversation. The biblical books and letters were addressed to specific people dealing with specific situations, but there is much about those people and situations that we simply don't know. If we knew all that had been said and done to prompt these biblical writings, we would understand the Bible much better. Some biblical passages sound strange to us because we didn't hear the question or live through the circumstance that prompted them.

That is probably the case in these verses. When John writes, "This is the one who came by water and blood, Jesus Christ, not with water only, but with water and blood (5:6)" it sounds like gobbledygook to us. When he goes on to say, "There are three that testify: the Spirit and the water and the blood, and these three agree" (5:8), we're not sure what he's referring to. We long for the other side of the conversation so we can have some context for these verses.

There is little doubt that Gnosticism, once again, is the backdrop for these verses. John was probably addressing a particular brand of Gnosticism called Cerinthian Gnosticism, which was named after Cerinthus, a contemporary of John's. Cerinthus taught that, at Jesus' baptism, the divine spirit entered Jesus in the form of a dove. Jesus then lived a perfect, divine life that pointed people to God. But then, Cerinthus maintained, the divine spirit departed Jesus sometime before the cross so that a very human Jesus, without the divine spirit, died there. In other words, for Cerinthus, the spirit came to Jesus by water (the baptism) but not by blood (the cross).

When John asserts that Jesus came by water *and* by blood, he is affirming the importance of the cross. Contrary to what Cerinthus was teaching, Jesus was just as much God at the cross as he was at the baptism. The Spirit, the water, and the blood are all vital to who Jesus was, and to downplay any of them is to downplay the truth about Jesus. The Spirit, the baptism, and the cross all sing in unison, declaring that Jesus was God's Son.

Then John reiterates the importance of holding on to the truth of Christ and rejecting the falsehoods of the gnostics: "Those who believe in the Son of God have the testimony in their hearts. Those who do not believe in God have made him a liar by not believing in the testimony God has given concerning his Son" (5:10-11). And what exactly is this testimony that God has given us concerning his Son? How do we know we have the real thing and not a "knock-off" of true faith?

Here's John's response: "And this is the testimony: God gave us eternal life, and this life is in his Son. Whoever has the Son has life; whoever does not have the Son does not have life" (5:11-12). John's answer to the question about the authenticity of faith can be summed up in one word: *Life.* If we really have Jesus, we have life. And if we don't have Jesus, we don't have life.

When John uses the phrase "eternal life," he has something more in mind than just living forever. Eternal life describes quality as much as it describes quantity. God gives us eternal life, a divinely blessed life that begins now and continues beyond death. In *The Letters of John*, William Hendricks describes it like this:

Clues to the Positive Content of Eternal Life

Inklings about the dimensions of eternal life abound in the Gospel. Among them we name the following:
1. satisfaction of spiritual thirst (4:14; 6:35)
2. everlasting life (4:14; 6:40, 51, 54; 12:25)
3. light for life (8:12)
4. abundant life (10:10)
5. knowledge of God (17:3)
6. transference out of a deathly existence into a new realm (5:24)
7. a gracious gift of God (6:33; 10:28; 17:2)

It is a distortion of John's thought to place eternal life only in the future. *Now* we are sons and daughters of God. *Now* his life is in us. Christ came to bring life to the cosmos. Those who are Christ's should be lively and loving. It is Christ himself who sustains them; he is their water, their bread, their nurturing vine—their life. Far from denying the individual personality, such nourishment enhances it. The message of John is that God wants to liven up people to be what they were intended to be. Through Christ God has been bringing new creations into being. In the Spirit a new breath has blown into the arena of human existence. Whoever has the Son, has life; whoever does not have the Son does not have life."[3]

In 1866, Algernon Charles Swinburne published a poem titled "Hymn to Proserpine." The poem lamented the rise of Christianity and had one line that read, "Thou hast conquered, O pale Galilean, and the world has grown grey from thy breath."

John would have agreed with the first part of that line: Jesus has indeed conquered the world. But he would have disagreed vehemently with the second part: the world has not grown gray because of his influence; it has grown colorful and joyful. Those who know "the pale Galilean" have received eternal life, a life that is vibrant and passionate. Christians are not supposed to be gray. After all, we're following one who said, "I came that they may have life, and have it abundantly" (John 10:10).

Let the words of Eugene Peterson in *Traveling Light* echo John's words about Jesus as the giver of life:

> The word *Christian* means different things to different people. To one person it means a stiff, uptight, inflexible way of life, colorless and unbending. To another it means a risky, surprise-filled venture, lived tiptoe at the edge of expectation. Either of these pictures can be supported with evidence. There are numberless illustrations for either position in congregations all over the world. But if we restrict ourselves to biblical evidence, only the second image can be supported: the image of the person living zestfully, exploring every experience—pain and joy, enigma and insight, fulfillment and frustration—as a dimension of human freedom, searching through each for sense and grace. If we get our information from the biblical material, there is no doubt that the Christian life is a dancing, leaping, daring life.[4]

John said essentially the same thing in six powerful words: "Whoever has the Son has life." Jesus is the source of real life. Those who plug into him get energy, passion, and joy. Those who don't plug into him are missing out on the divine power source that God has provided to all who will avail themselves of it.

It may well be that Swinburne's "pale Galilean" and "grey world" are accurate descriptions of much Christianity in the world. Ellen Glasgow, in her autobiography, describes her father, a somber and rigid Presbyterian elder, like this: "He was entirely unselfish, and in his entire life he never committed a pleasure."[5]

If we take these verses in John seriously, we will most definitely be entirely unselfish. But if we take these verses in John seriously, we will also feel free to commit a pleasure or two.

THE CAUSE FOR OUR CONFIDENCE (5:13-17)

Earlier I mentioned that John uses the word *know* thirty-nine times in this letter. There was good reason for that. The Christians in Ephesus were not sure what they knew for certain anymore. The gnostics were teaching some things about Jesus that shook their faith. On top of that, they were growing disillusioned about some of the truths they had always believed. They were wondering if this faith handed to them by their parents and grandparents was really true.

John knew he was writing to a church in need of truth, a church that needed to reestablish some anchors in a turbulent world. The Christians in Ephesus didn't just need to think, wonder, speculate, or hope; they needed to *know*. They needed their confidence restored so that they could live with passion again.

As he comes to the end of his letter to them, John asserts three things that followers of Jesus can know with confidence.

First, *we can have confidence in our relationship with God.* His purpose for writing the letter in the first place, John says, was to show the Christians in Ephesus that they could be confident in their standing with God: "I write these things to you who believe in the name of the Son of God, so that you may know that you have eternal life" (5:13). They didn't have to wonder about their relationship with God; they could know for certain they had eternal life.

I went through a miserable time when I was in college, doubting my salvation. I became a Christian when I was a young boy and grew up in the church. My conversion experience was nothing like the Apostle Paul's—no voices from heaven, no blinding lights, nothing spectacular at all. I just grew up in a Christian home and made a child-like step of faith at an early age.

But during my freshman year in college I started doubting that experience. "How much can a little boy know about the cost of discipleship?" I wondered. Maybe that conversion experience wasn't valid after all. Maybe I needed to make another decision, now that I was older, and be baptized a second time. For several months, I doubted my salvation and lived in the agony of uncertainty. I didn't have the confidence John wrote about. I didn't know for certain that I had eternal life.

Fortunately, perhaps providentially, I saw an article in our local newspaper that had an interview with Ruth Graham, Billy Graham's wife. The interviewer asked her if she remembered the exact moment she had become a Christian, and she said she did not. Then she added the line I needed to hear: "Just because you can't remember your birthday doesn't mean you weren't born."

That sentence was music to my doubting ears. I had been focusing solely on my spiritual birthday and concerned only about what had happened—or hadn't happened—twelve years earlier. But the real questions should have been these: Do I have a relationship with God *now*? Do I know for certain that I have eternal life *now*? I knew the answers to those questions were a resounding "yes" and put my doubts away for good. I came to see my early, less-than-spectacular conversion as a first step on a long journey of learning and discovery. True, I didn't know much when I made that first decision, but I knew enough to start the journey.

That experience showed me the misery of having to live in an uncertain relationship with God—a condition I'm afraid most of society is in. Ask the average man, woman, boy, or girl on the street, "Do you know that you have a relationship with God? Do you know that you have eternal life?" and they will likely answer, "I hope so."

That answer is usually based on a "works theology." Most people have the idea that if their good deeds outnumber their bad deeds during their sojourn on this earth, God will smile on them and welcome them into heaven. If, on the other hand, their bad deeds outnumber their good deeds, God will have to turn them away. The reason for their "I hope so" answer is that they're not sure what the eternal scale will reveal. Maybe their good deeds will outweigh their bad ones, and up they will go. But then again, maybe not. Only time—and God—will tell.

Notice again John's wording in 1 John 5:13. He doesn't say, "I write these things to you whose good deeds surely outnumber your bad deeds, so that you may know that you have eternal life." He says, "I write these things to you who believe in the name of the Son of God, so that you may know that you have eternal life." The issue is not good or bad deeds; the issue is believing in the name of the Son of God. In other words, those who know and trust the finished work of Christ can live with confidence: "Therefore there is now no condemnation for those who are in Christ Jesus. For the law of the Spirit of life in Christ Jesus has set you free from the law of sin and death" (Rom 8:2). Set free, Paul exults. From the law of sin and death. From a purposeless existence. And from the agony of uncertainty in our relationship with God.

Hallelujah! Because of what Christ has already done, we can live with confidence that we have eternal life.

Second, *we can have confidence that God answers prayer.* Let's be honest. We're not sure *how* prayer works, and sometimes we're not even sure *if* prayer works. Prayer is the ultimate mystery, and to try to make it simple and understandable is to reduce beautiful poetry to pedantic prose.

But as John closes his letter, he tells the Ephesians to pray confidently and boldly to God: "And this is the boldness we have in him, that if we ask anything according to his will, he hears us. And if we know that he hears us in whatever we ask, we know that we have obtained the requests made of him" (5:14-15). That might sound a bit overstated, except for the fact that Jesus himself said similar things (see Matt 18:19, 21:21; Mk 11:24; John 14:14).

Those promises about getting whatever we ask for when we pray sound wonderful, but they run headlong into two major obstacles: (1) our personal experience with prayer and (2) a number of the biblical characters' experience with prayer. As for our personal experience with prayer, most of us have prayed fervently for sick people to get well, failing marriages to get better, quarreling people to find reconciliation, and a host of other noble causes. We assumed God wanted those things to happen, too, so we assumed we were in sync with God's desire. But, to the great detriment of our faith, they didn't happen. When we read these glowing passages about prayer in the Bible, we have to admit that they don't match up with our own experience.

And many of the people in the Bible didn't get what they prayed for either. Moses prayed to get to enter the promised land with his people. David prayed that his infant son wouldn't die. The armies of Israel prayed for victory over their enemies. Habakkuk prayed for deliverance from the Babylonians. Jeremiah prayed that Jerusalem wouldn't be destroyed. Jesus prayed that he wouldn't have to die. Paul prayed for a "thorn in the flesh" to be removed. None of those requests was granted. So, while the Bible tells us to pray with confidence, expecting God to answer, it also gives us many examples of people who prayed and didn't receive what they prayed for.

It is worth noting that John does put a stipulation on answered prayer: "If we ask anything according to his will, he hears us" (5:14b). The prayer that gets answered is the one prayed "according to his will." That one stipulation means that not all of our prayers will be answered simply because they're not in line with God's will. Surprisingly, God may not want us to have the new Lexus, for our son to make the all-star team, or for us to get the job promotion. *We* want those things, for sure, but God may not. A wise and mature God, in other words, may not choose to answer our silly and immature requests.

The requirement that we pray according to God's will makes us look at ourselves and our understanding of God. Do we even know enough about God to have a clue what his will might be? In his book *Prayer: Does It Make Any Difference?*, Philip Yancey quotes David Mains regarding a checklist we can use to make sure our prayers are on target:

• *What do I really want?* Am I being specific, or am I just rambling about nothing in particular?
• *Can God grant this request?* Or is it against God's nature to do so?
• *Have I done my part?* Or am I praying to lose weight when I haven't dieted?
• *How is my relationship with God?* Are we on speaking terms?
• *Who will get the credit if my request is granted?* Do I have God's interests in mind?
• *Do I really want my prayer answered?* What would really happen if God granted my request?[6]

As we ask those kinds of questions, we gradually build a partnership with God that allows us to discern what God wants to accomplish on earth. We learn God's will, in other words, and we begin to pray accordingly.

In his book, Yancey also includes this prayer by the British writer John Baillie that seems to me to be the kind of prayer that is in harmony with the will of God:

Teach me, O God, to use all the circumstances of my life today
that they may bring forth in me the fruits of holiness rather
than the fruits of sin.
Let me use disappointment as material for patience.
Let me use success as material for thankfulness.
Let me use trouble as material for perseverance.
Let me use danger as material for courage.
Let me use reproach as material for long suffering.
Let me use praise as material for humility.
Let me use pleasure as material for temperance.
Let me use pain as material for endurance.[7]

Not only is that kind of prayer in line with the character and will of God, it is
also the kind of prayer that God always answers.

The assumption underneath those glowing promises about prayer is not
to be missed, though. The reason we are to come confidently before God is
that God is *for* us. God wants to bless us. God wants to give good gifts to us.
Remember Jesus' famous invitation to prayer in the Sermon on the Mount?

> Ask, and it will be given you; search, and you will find; knock, and the door
> will be opened for you. For everyone who asks receives, and everyone who
> searches finds, and for everyone who knocks, the door will be opened. Is there
> anyone among you who, if your child asks for bread, will give a stone? Of if
> the child asks for a fish, will give a snake? If you then, who are evil, know how
> to give good gifts to your children, how much more will your Father in heaven
> give good gifts to those who ask him? (Matt 7:7-11)

The reason we can ask, search, and knock with expectancy is that the One
we're approaching loves us beyond measure. Think how much we love our own
children. We would do anything for them. And if we, being evil, feel that way
about our kids, how much more will God, who is Infinite Love, feel that way
about us?

Therefore, ask, search, and knock with no hesitancy and with great
confidence. "And this is the boldness we have in him, that if we ask anything
according to his will, he hears us. And if we know that he hears us in whatever
we ask, we know that we have obtained the requests made of him" (5:4-15).

> Believe Somebody is listening. Believe in miracles. That's what Jesus told
> the father who asked him to heal his epileptic son. Jesus said, "All things are
> possible to him who believes." And the father spoke for all of us when he
> answered, "Lord, I believe; help my unbelief!" (Mk 9:14-29) What about
> when the boy is not healed? When, listened to or not listened to, the prayer
> goes unanswered? Who knows? Just keep praying, Jesus says. Remember the
> sleepy friend, the crooked judge. Even if the boy dies, keep on beating the path
> to God's door, because the one thing you can be sure of is that down the path
> you beat with even your most half-cocked and halting prayer the God you call
> upon will surely come, and even if he does not bring you the answer you want,
> he will bring you himself. And, maybe at the secret heart of all our prayers that
> is what we are really praying for.[8]

If Somebody is listening, and if our prayers enable us to sense God's presence and peace, then our prayers never really go unanswered. But, if we're honest, we must admit that at times if feels as if they do. I suspect the line of people waiting to ask God "Why?" stretches around the globe.

Third, *we can have confidence that God can change people.* While he is on the subject of confident prayer John adds, "If you see your brother or sister committing what is not a mortal sin, you will ask, and God will give life to such a one . . ." (5:16a). If his thought ended there, we would all celebrate the wonderful truth that our prayers on behalf of our brothers and sisters make a difference and enable God to give them new life. We would be encouraged to pray not only for physically sick people to get well but also for emotionally and spiritually sick people to get well.

But John's thought does not end there, and he goes on to write one of the most troubling and hotly debated concepts in the letter of 1 John. We are to pray, he continues, for "those whose sin is not mortal. There is a sin that is mortal; I do not say that you should pray about that. All wrongdoing is sin, but there is sin that is not mortal" (5:16b-17).

In Greek, the sin John describes is *pros thanaton*, the sin *that is going toward death.* It seems to dovetail with the sin Jesus describes in Matthew 12:31: "Therefore I tell you, people will be forgiven for every sin and blasphemy, but blasphemy against the Holy Spirit will not be forgiven." What is this sin John and Jesus are describing? What is the one sin that is mortal, leading to death and unforgivable?

Though biblical interpreters have suggested many possibilities, the one that makes the most sense to me centers on Jesus' phrase "blasphemy against the Holy Spirit." The Holy Spirit is God's agent for leading us to truth and love. The Spirit convicts us of sin and shows us a better way to live. But it is possible to become so hardened and confused that we can no longer sense the Spirit's promptings. We can become so hardened and confused, in fact, that good looks bad and darkness seems to be light.

I once read an article about scientists who were studying fish living in the dark recesses of Mammoth Cave. The scientists made an interesting discovery about those fish. Though they had eyes, they were completely blind. Darkness had been their home for so long that they could no longer detect light.

When that happens to us morally and spiritually, perhaps we have crossed the line and committed the unforgivable sin, the sin that leads to death. Once we no longer have spiritual eyes to sense God's love and truth, we have put ourselves in a hopeless situation. God can't reach us because we no longer have eyes to see or ears to hear.

We've grown so hardened and confused that darkness seems normal and light seems blinding.

Occasionally, we read about terrorists who kill in the name of God. Their God wants infidels murdered, and these terrorists think they will be rewarded in the afterlife if they are "faithful" to God's commands to kill. Consider the convoluted, upside-down thinking of those terrorists. In their minds, God wants people killed, other people are infidels deserving of death, and those who are the most

Typical Identifications of the Sin unto Death

1. Acceptance of heretical doctrine or wanton transgression of divine commandment (Bultmann)
2. Heinous sins for which there is no pardon, such as murder (3:15), idolatry (5:21), injustice, apostasy, adultery, fornication (Tertullian). (See *Jub.* 33:12-18.)
3. An over-rigorous application of the unpardonable sin (Mark 3:28-29) in the heat of controversy (Dodd)
4. Christ-rejecting behavior and implicit rejection of the atonement. See Tim Ward, "Sin 'Not Unto Death' and Sin 'Unto Death' in 1 John 5," *Churchman* 109 (1995): 236–37.
5. The secessionists who denied Jesus Christ come in the flesh (Brown)
6. Mortal sin as distinguished from venial (less serious, pardonable) sins (Roman Catholic tradition)
7. Any sin that deliberately rejects the claims of Christ persistently (Brooke)
8. Sins incompatible with being a child of God: denial of Jesus Christ as Son of God, refusal to obey commands of God, love of the world, and hatred of one's fellow believers (Marshall)

"faithful" in killing others will be rewarded in heaven. Their definitions of God, faith, commitment, and eternal rewards are completely upside down. They have transformed all things good into all things bad. Like the fish in Mammoth Cave, they have grown so used to the darkness that they can no longer see light.

It is one of the sad realities of the human condition that our sinful, convoluted thinking can come to seem normal, even virtuous, to us. We can become so blind to the truth that falsehood looks truthful, hateful deeds look righteous, and the devil himself looks like God. When the Spirit tries to draw us to real truth, we're too blind to see and too confused to understand.

Occasionally, sincere Christians will be fearful that they have perhaps committed the unforgivable sin. The irony is that anyone concerned about committing the unforgivable sin hasn't done it. Anyone concerned about God and righteousness is obviously still able to see the light. Anyone concerned about God and righteousness is still open to the Holy Spirit.

John's detour into the subject of "mortal sin" obscures the truth we should be celebrating, though. Our prayers on behalf of our brothers and sisters do make a difference. God can take those prayers and use them to heal people emotionally and spiritually. As we pray with confidence, we can also be confident that our prayers for our family members and friends will help God change their lives.

In his desire to help us understand the difference Jesus makes in a person's life, John says that Christ is the cause of our confidence. Because of him, we can be confident in our relationship with God, confident in bringing our prayers to God, and confident that God can use our prayers to change others.

THE KEY TO OUR UNDERSTANDING (5:18-21)

John ends his letter by once again featuring the word *know*. Three times he uses the phrase *we know* to underscore three more truths the Ephesian Christians should hold fast in their minds and hearts:

• "We know that those who are born of God do not sin, but the one who was born of God protects them, and the evil one does not touch them" (5:18). Mark it down: those who know God do not habitually and consistently choose to sin. Christians will most definitely sin, but they will not be happy about it. The Spirit will be constantly reminding them to get back on the Way, and "the one who is in them is greater than the one who is in the world" (4:4).

• "We know that we are God's children, and that the whole world lies under the power of the evil one" (5:19). Mark it down: those who know God are on a countercultural journey that places them on a narrow road. Their attitudes, goals, relationships, and actions are radically different than those of the people around them. As Paul put it to the Corinthians, "So if anyone is in Christ, there is a new creation: everything old has passed away; see everything has become new!" (2 Cor 5:17).

• "And we know that the Son has come and has given us understanding so that we may know him who is true, and we are in him who is true, in his Son Jesus Christ. He is the true God and eternal life" (5:20). Mark it down: those who know God know that Jesus Christ leads us to the real and true life and that he is the key to understanding reality. When we come to Christ, we get a different pattern by which to live our lives, and we start to filter everything through the lens of Jesus. He becomes our key to understanding life.

Let's focus our attention on the third of those truths: Christ as the key to seeing and understanding life. Several years ago, the question "What would Jesus do?" became popular in evangelical circles. People wore "WWJD?" bracelets, necklaces, and T-shirts. The question almost became trite, a sales gimmick that reduced the Christian Way to a clever slogan.

But that question was not trite at all. After we come to Christ, we consistently ask ourselves that question because he becomes our Lord, and we've pledged to follow him. Following him means we try to adopt his priorities and walk in his footsteps. Though we may never feel inclined to emblazon it on a t-shirt, we're constantly asking ourselves the question, "What would Jesus do?"

In the New Testament, the Greek word *mathetes* appears 269 times. The word is usually translated "disciple." It means one who is a pupil or learner. A *mathetes* apprentices himself or herself to another to learn a craft or trade. In the biblical usage, a *mathetes* apprentices himself or herself to Jesus Christ. Some in the first-century world would apprentice themselves to someone to learn how to sew, fish, farm, or cook. Christians, though, apprentice themselves to Jesus Christ to learn how to *live*.

One time Jesus gathered his apprentices together and gave them a crash course in Christian Living 101. Ever since he delivered that course on the mountainside, we Christian apprentices have been going back to it to learn how to live. He talked about happiness, influence, anger, adultery, divorce, honesty, revenge, grace, giving, prayer, fasting, money, worry, relationships, and commitment. In short, in the Sermon on the Mount he addressed just about everything that matters.

At the end of that course on Christian Living 101, Jesus told the story of two houses—one built on a foundation of sand and one built on a foundation of rock. Those who ignore his counsel, he said, are building their lives on sand, and when the storms come, their houses will fall. But those who hear his words and follow them are building their life houses on rock, and when the storms come they will stand firm, anchored on a strong foundation.

Ever since Jesus gave that class on Christian Living 101, we apprentices have been going back to it to remind ourselves who we are and how we're supposed to be living. He spelled out a new blueprint for living human life, and, though it might seem strange to many people, it is the true and real life, as John says in 1 John. It is the blueprint for "life more abundant" (Jn 10:10).

I'll never forget the day I got my first pair of glasses. I was in the fourth grade, and an eye exam at school had indicated my vision wasn't what it should be. My parents took me to the optometrist's office, and, sure enough, he said I needed glasses. When the glasses arrived, I went again to his office, and he put them on me and told me to look out the window. I could scarcely believe what I saw. The trees had distinct leaves. The people had distinct faces. The cars had distinct license plates. I had been seeing out of faulty eyes for a long time and didn't even know it. When I put those glasses on, all things became new.

When John writes about Jesus being the key to understanding life, he's alluding to a similar phenomenon. When we follow Christ, we start to see life through new eyes. Without him, we're doomed to fuzzy, faulty vision. But with him, we get new clarity. We begin to see what matters, what is truthful, what is real. It is not overstating the case to say that sin is what happens when we take our glasses off, and abundant living is what happens when we put them on. Christ is the key to understanding life and the one who can keep us focused on what matters most.

John ends 1 John with this final admonition: "Little children, keep yourselves from idols" (5:21). He may have been speaking literally, for Ephesus was known as a city of many idols and the home of the great Temple of Diana, one of the wonders of the ancient world. John may have been warning the Ephesian Christians to avoid idols and stay away from pagan temples.

But he may have been speaking more generally, telling them to shun all false gods and to hold to Christ, who is the way, the truth, and the life. Idols come in many shapes and sizes. In fact, an idol is any person, place, or thing we pledge our allegiance to, any ultimate concern that preempts God. In light of his final plea to the Ephesians to make Christ the key to their understanding of life, John may have been telling them to let that keep happening. Let Christ continue to be their pattern for living. Let Christ continue to be the glasses through which they see the world. Let Christ continue to show them the truth, for in following his truth they will be set free.

CONCLUSION

As we have seen, the Ephesians at the end of the first century were dealing with a couple of heavy problems. They were dealing with disillusionment and wondering if the Christian Way, passed on to them from their parents and grandparents, was really true. They needed someone to assure them of the truth of this Way.

They were also dealing with doctrinal confusion, as the gnostics were saying some things about Jesus that they had not heard before. The Ephesians were confused about who Jesus was and needed someone to assure them about his true nature and work.

John wrote 1 John to speak to both of those problems. In chapter 5, he writes practically about the difference Jesus makes in a person's life and, in the process, addresses both issues the Ephesians were grappling with. In spelling out the difference Jesus makes, John *informs* them about the nature of Christ and also *inspires* them to hold fast to him.

Imagine, if you can, a world without Jesus Christ. No birth in Bethlehem. No teachings, parables, or Sermon on the Mount. No clash with the religious legalists of his day. No cross at Golgotha. No empty tomb three days later. No appearances to his disciples after the resurrection. If there were not a Jesus of Nazareth in human history, all those things would not have happened. But, according to John in 1 John 5, we would also be lacking some key ingredients in our quest to live abundantly.

- We would be lacking direction and joy because Christ is *the reason for our victory*. Because of the cross and resurrection, we won! And we get to live as victorious people.
- We would be lacking power and passion because Christ is *the source of our life*. When we're connected to him, the Christian life is a dancing, leaping, daring adventure.
- We would be lacking expectancy and assurance because Christ is *the cause for our confidence*. We can know that we have eternal life, that God answers prayer, and that God changes people's lives.
- We would be lacking direction and purpose because Christ is *the key to our understanding*. Once we start taking Jesus seriously, we get a new vision of life, a new understanding of what is real and true.

Of course, there *is* a Jesus of Nazareth in human history and in our own lives. Because of that, we get to claim all four of those grand promises in 1 John 5. If we happen to be confused or disillusioned, John invites us to look again at Christ—at what he has done in our lives already and what he would like to do in our lives in the future. In a world not all that different from first-century Ephesus, he invites us to reclaim our allegiance to Christ, to stand and sing with renewed conviction: "On Christ the solid rock I stand, all other ground is sinking sand."

QUESTIONS FOR REFLECTION AND DISCUSSION

1. Do you believe we now live in a mix-and-match world where people try to create their own religion? What do you think of John's use of the word "know"? How do we balance conviction with acceptance of others?

2. Do you agree that the Christian Way sometimes seems burdensome? What does the typical non-churchgoer think about church?

3. Had you ever thought of eternal life as something that begins *now*—before we die? Do you think most people see Christianity as "pale" and "grey"?

4. Have you ever doubted your conversion experience? How did you resolve that dilemma?

5. How do you deal with the problem of unanswered prayer? Do you pray with confidence?

6. What is the unpardonable sin, the sin that leads to death?

7. In what specific ways does Christ change our understanding of life? Did you find the slogan *"What would Jesus do?"* helpful or offensive? How can we know what Jesus would do in any situation?

8. In chapter 5, John mentions four differences Jesus makes in a person's life. Can you think of others? Are there other ways Christ has changed your life?

SUGGESTIONS FOR WORSHIP AND PREACHING

An Order of Worship

This worship service is centered on the last few verses in 1 John. These verses remind us that Christ come to give us a new understanding of life. When we come to Christ, "we are in him who is true" (5:20), and we start to get a new perspective on the truth. This service will encourage worshipers to stay true to Christ and not be conformed to popular culture.

The Worship of God

"And we know that the Son of God has come and has given us understanding so that we may know him who is true . . ." (1 John 5:20a).

Spoken Call to Worship

The Chiming of the Hour

Hymn: "Crown Him with Many Crowns"

Invocation

Children's Time

Hymn: "O for a Thousand Tongues to Sing"

Receiving Tithes and Offerings

Offertory Prayer

The Word of the Lord: 1 John 5:19-20

　　Worship Leader: This is the word of the Lord.

　　Congregation: Thanks be to God.

Anthem: "With Every Breath" (Ken Medema, copyright 1993 by Shawnee Press)

Sermon: "Looking at the World with New Glasses"

Hymn of Response: "Redeemed"

Choral Benediction: "Yours Is the Kingdom" (Cindy Berry, copyright 1999 by Shawnee Press)

Postlude

A Sermon Sketch: "Looking at the World with New Glasses" (1 John 5:19-20)

Introduction

Those of us who wear glasses or contacts know how handicapped we would be without them. When I take off my glasses, I can barely read the big "E" on the eye chart. I think I'm legally blind when I take my glasses off. I still remember when I got my first pair of glasses. I was in the fourth grade, and I couldn't believe how much better I could see when I put on those glasses for the first time. I put them on . . . and looked out at a whole new world.

All Things New

The New Testament writers tell us something like that happens when we start to follow Christ. The apostle Paul put it like this: "So if anyone is in Christ, there is a new creation: everything old has passed away; see everything has become new!" (2 Cor 5:17).

At the end of 1 John, John expresses the same idea: "And we know that the Son of God has come and has given us understanding so that we may know him who is true; and we are in him who is true, in his Son Jesus Christ. He is the true God and eternal life" (1 Jn 5:20).

Once we come to Christ, Paul and John are telling us, we start to see the world with new glasses. Everything becomes new. We know him who is true and start to see the world from a different perspective.

Christian Living 101

The Greek word *mathetes* appears 269 times in the New Testament. It is usually translated "disciple" and refers to one who apprentices himself of herself to a master teacher. When we decide to follow Christ, we start to walk in his footsteps, listen to his instructions, and look at life the way he saw life.

He has given us plenty of material, too. The Sermon on the Mount alone is enough to keep us busy for a lifetime. In that sermon Jesus addressed some of the most essential and practical dimensions of life. He spoke about happiness, influence, anger, adultery, divorce, honesty, revenge, grace, giving, prayer, fasting, money, worry, relationships, and commitment. By the time we absorb his wisdom on those issues, we're looking at the world in a new way. We're no longer conformed to this world, but we're transformed by the renewing of our minds (see Rom 12:2).

Finding Our Way
On a trip years ago, I lost my glasses. My trip was pretty much ruined. I couldn't read, watch television, drive a car, go to a movie, or do any of the ordinary activities I usually take for granted.

God, in his love and mercy, has given us truth in Christ. When we learn his truth and follow that truth, we get a new way of coming at life, a way Jesus called "life more abundant" (Jn 10:10). As long as we have those glasses on, John says in our text this morning, we're able to see and live the truth. We're able to live abundantly because our vision is clear. Where in the world would we be, though, without those glasses?

NOTES

1. Eugene Peterson, *Traveling Light* (Downers Grove IL: InterVarsity Press, 1982) 49.

2. William Barclay, *The Letters of John and Jude* (Louisville: Westminster John Knox Press, 1976) 106.

3. William Hendricks, *The Letters of John* (Nashville: Convention Press, 1970) 137.

4. Peterson, *Traveling Light*, 57.

5. Ellen Glasgow, *The Woman Within* (New York: Harcourt, Brace, and Co., 1954) 15.

6. Philip Yancey, *Prayer: Does It Make Any Difference?* (Grand Rapids MI: Zondervan, 2006) 226.

7. Ibid, 240.

8. Frederick Buechner, *Wishful Thinking* (New York: Harper & Row, 1973) 71.

THE TRUTH ABOUT BAD RELIGION

Focal Text—2 & 3 John, Jude

Charles Kimball begins his book *When Religion Becomes Evil* with these words:

> Religion is arguably the most powerful and pervasive force on earth. Throughout history religious ideas and commitments have inspired individuals and communities of faith to transcend narrow self-interest in pursuit of higher values and truths. The record of history shows noble acts of love, self-sacrifice, and service to others frequently rooted in deeply held religious world views. At the same time, history clearly shows that religion has often been linked directly to the worst examples of human behavior. It is somewhat trite, but nevertheless sadly true, to say that more wars have been waged, more people killed, and these days more evil perpetrated in the name of religion than by any other institutional force in human history.[1]

Most of us don't have to read that in a book to know it is true; we've experienced that truth in our own lives. We've experienced the church at its best—proclaiming the good news, ministering to the hungry and hurting, providing community in a fragmented world, worshiping in deep and meaningful ways, and providing strength and peace when life gets hard. Sometimes, when we think about the place of the church in our lives, we find ourselves praying, "Thank you, God, for the church!"

We have also experienced the church at its worst—arguing over trivial issues, building walls instead of bridges, spewing easy answers to hard questions, becoming more concerned about institutional success than ministering to people and turning the good news of the gospel into the bad news of religion. Sometimes, when we think about the place of the church in our lives, we find ourselves praying, "Deliver me, God, from the church!"

This situation is not unique to our time in history. The church has always been a mixed bag of good and bad. When Jesus addressed the seven churches of Asia Minor as recorded in the book of Revelation, he typically offered them a word of *commendation* followed by a word of *condemnation*. He found things in those churches worthy of praise, but he also found things in those churches worthy of criticism. Like our churches today, those first-century churches were "Thank you/deliver me" congregations.

Our final session in this study focuses on 2 and 3 John and Jude, which all have something to say about bad religion. Each of these one-chapter books addresses a different problem in the church, but they all deal with bad religion, ways the church was falling short in its life and ministry. Second John speaks to the problem of *bad teaching*. Third John deals with *bad leadership*, and Jude addresses *bad living*. Both problems are ongoing in our churches today.

It is likely that you have never studied these three little books before. The reason, I suspect, is that they're seen as "negative," and few of us like to dwell on the negative. We also are not fond of being criticized, and 2 and 3 John and Jude are critical in tone. They were written to address specific problems, but who wants to dwell on problems? Who wants others to point out our flaws? We often skip these negative letters in favor of something more edifying, like the Gospels or the letters of Paul.

But if the shoe happens to fit, we need to be willing to wear it. If we've stumbled into bad religion, it would be helpful if someone would point it out to us—even if we cringe to hear it. Let's brace ourselves for the plainspoken words of John and Jude as they speak candidly about bad religion. Let's open our minds to the truth about bad religion—even if it hurts to hear it.

BAD TEACHING (2 JOHN)

John addresses his second epistle to "the elect lady and her children" (v. 1). Some scholars think he was writing to a woman who led a house church in or around Ephesus. The consensus, though, seems to be that "the elect lady" is a reference to a church, not a person. It was not uncommon in biblical days to personify churches and to speak of their members as "children" as John does here.

We have no idea which church John was writing to, but we do know he loved the church dearly. He loved these people in the truth, he declares, as did others who knew and loved the truth about Jesus that had transformed all their lives. Notice, once again, John's emphasis on the truth. As in 1 John, he is focused on learning and living the truth.

A Beginning Benediction (vv. 1-3)

Then John offers these people a beginning benediction, which is not just a "last word" but also a "good word." We think of a benediction as a closing prayer, but it is a good word that can be spoken at any time, and John puts his benediction at the beginning of his letter. It goes like this: "Grace, mercy, and peace will be with us from God the Father and from Jesus Christ, the Father's Son, in truth and love" (v. 3).

Unlike most benedictions, this one is not a wish or prayer; it is a promise. John is not *hoping* the people will find grace, mercy, and peace from God; he is *promising* it. Grace, mercy, and peace *will* be with them, he writes. And how will this grace, mercy, and peace come into their lives? It will arrive "in truth and love" (v. 3b). The more truth they learn and live, and the more love they receive and give away, the more grace, mercy, and peace they will experience. A positive cycle is set in place: the more they receive the more they give, and then the more they give the more they receive, and so on. Life goes spiraling upward.

This beginning benediction presents an intriguing notion about the rhythm in a life of faith. Many of us know what it's like to find our rhythm on the golf course, in a presentation at work, or when writing a book or article. Sometimes, we just "get in the flow" and do surprising things—shoot par, give a flawless presentation, or write a stunning paragraph. When we find our rhythm, we're amazed how well we do and how good life is.

The life of faith has a rhythm to it as well, and when we find it, we're amazed at how blessed we are and how gracious God is. The rhythm begins when we experience the grace, mercy, and peace of God, as John says here. This is the first note in the rhythm of faith, and it fills us with both gratitude and joy.

The second note in the rhythm of faith is the one John is preparing to write about in the next verses: giving this grace, mercy, and peace to others. As we will shortly see, John once again stresses the idea of "loving one another" in verses 4-6. He spent much of 1 John speaking about loving others, and here in 2 John he sounds that note again. We are to take the grace, mercy, and peace we have received from God and live in truth and love. Freely we have received, and freely we give.

In one of his sermons, Fred Craddock told of an experience he had during a trip for a speaking engagement in Wyoming. He said that when he left his home in Atlanta, it was warm, and he didn't pack a jacket. When he arrived in Wyoming, his host picked him up at the airport and drove him to his conference. On the way, though, his friend wanted to stop at a scenic overlook so Craddock could appreciate the beauty of the Wyoming landscape. They stopped, and the friend pointed out some of the awesome mountains in the distance—and even some antelope racing across the countryside. Craddock said it was beautiful, but there was one small problem: he was freezing! It was a lot colder in Wyoming than it had been in Atlanta.

He said that as he stood shivering on the overlook, a woman sidled up beside him, slipped a sweater around his shoulders, and whispered, "You'll enjoy it more if you wear this." And, wonder of wonders, he said, she was right. Once he had that sweater on, the view was much better. The awesome mountains. The graceful antelope. It was a magnificent place to be. Craddock said he noticed the woman who had given him the sweater preparing to leave, so he took the sweater off and tried to give it back to her. "Just keep it and pass it along," she said.

As he and his friend prepared to leave the overlook, Craddock noticed a young woman and her boyfriend trying to enjoy the view, too. But she was short-sleeved and shivering and having a hard time appreciating the beauty. Craddock took the sweater, gently placed it around her shoulders, and said, "You'll enjoy it more if your wear this." And he and his friend left.

> ### The Elder's Scope of Authority
> The fact that the writer of 2 John speaks with an air of authority to a congregation other than his own possibly suggests that he had general responsibility for all the Johannine churches in his area (so Williams, 66).
> Stephen Smalley, *1, 2, 3 John* (WBC; vol. 51; Waco TX: Word Books, 1984), 336.

Craddock concluded that story by saying he hoped that sweater is still up there on the scenic overlook, being passed from one cold shoulder to the next. Freely they all received, and freely they all gave.

That's a fine illustration of the rhythm of faith and a good way to understand this beginning benediction in 2 John. It begins by receiving the gifts of God: grace, mercy, and peace. But then, as we live with truth and love, we pass that grace, mercy, and peace on to others. What a paradise we would have if all people could live with the rhythm of faith. Freely we would receive the blessings of God, and freely we would pass them along to others.

Hard of Hearing and Struggling to Walk (vv. 4-6)

John is getting ready to say some hard things about false teachers in the church, but before he does, he tempers his words with this reminder about loving others: "Let us love one another" (v. 5b). As we saw in our sessions on 1 John, this was a recurring theme in John's writing—both in the Gospel of John and in these epistles.

Here he hints at two problems we encounter in trying to obey this command to love others. First, we tend to be hard of hearing when it comes to this command because it is "old hat." As John admits, this is not "a new commandment, but one we have had from the beginning"
(v. 5). Let the preacher thunder a message on loving others, and the congregation will yawn and give drowsy nods of agreement. There might even be a mumbled "Amen" or two. Then the basses in the choir will slip into hidden slumber, and the teenagers will go back to playing tic-tac-toe on the bulletin. Talk of love is boring because we've heard it all our lives.

As we saw in our second session on "The Truth about Loving People," Jesus did make loving others part of the greatest commandment in all the Law. Reduced to its essence, he said, Christianity is about loving God and loving people. Even though that might be "old hat" to us now, it is still the Great Commandment.

Think, though, of the some of the other great commandments we are prone to substitute in its place:

• "The great commandment," we say, "is being doctrinally sound. If you want to follow Jesus, you need to know the four spiritual laws, be able to define substitutionary atonement, and have the correct millennial view." We don't say it that bluntly, of course, but we imply it.
• "The great commandment," we say, "is climbing the ladder of Christian piety. If you want to follow Jesus, you must worship, pray, read the Bible every day, tithe, and maybe even fast from time to time." We have a nifty checklist of pious activities that separate the sheep from the goats.
• "The great commandment," we say, "is building a successful church. We must enroll people, raise money, build buildings, preach sermons, and hire professional staff. The gates of hell cannot prevail against our efforts to build a great institution." We have equated the institutional church with the kingdom of God when the two are hardly synonymous.

Don't misunderstand and accuse me of throwing stones at some of our most sacred cows. I am all for being doctrinally literate, practicing genuine piety, and building strong churches. But I also know that, as important as those things are, they are not the Great Commandment.

We can be doctrinally perfect, practice piety from sunrise to sunset, and grow a huge church and never understand the indispensable kernel of the Christian faith. Unless we love God with all that we have and are, and unless we love others as we love ourselves, we have missed the essence of it all. Though we have memorized the millennial chart, rubbed calluses on our knees in the prayer closet, and built churches with impressive statistics, if we have not love, we are as sounding brass or a tinkling cymbal.

If we let this old commandment to love others become "old hat" to us, we might continue to do our Christian activities, but we will lose the heart and soul of our faith.

John implies in these verses that we can fail to love others because this is an old commandment that we no longer have ears to hear.

Resources for Detailed Analysis of Verses 4-6

Raymond Brown, *The Epistles of John* (AB 30; Garden City NY: Doubleday, 1982), 660–68.

Ignace de la Potterie. *La Verite dans Saint Jean*. AnBib 73–74 (1977): 646–55.

U. C. von Wahlde. "The Theological Foundation of the Presbyter's Argument in 2 Jn (2 Jn 4-6)." *ZNW* 70 (1985): 209–24.

He also implies that we can fail to love others because we struggle to "walk the talk." He writes, "And this is love, that we walk according to his commandments; this is the commandment just as you heard it from the beginning—you must walk in it" (v. 6).

It's one thing to know we should love others; it's something else to "walk in it," to translate our knowledge into action. Remember John's words back in 1 John 3:18? "Little children, let us love, not in word or speech, but in truth and action." Here in 2 John, he doesn't say to *feel* love or *talk* love; he says to *walk* in love.

Occasionally, we read articles and books that tell us we need to say "I love you" more than we do. They remind us that our loved ones need to hear us speak our love, and I suspect there's some truth to that. But I must confess that I have a soft spot in my heart for those shy, not-as-verbal people who feel ill at ease spewing "I love you" on everybody. If they *live* their "I love you," that's good enough for me.

Real love is costly. It costs time, money, heartache, frustration, and worry. I realized early on as a husband and parent that what I *did* with my wife and children was more crucial that what I *said* to them. They needed me to speak my love, I knew, but they really needed me to walk my love.

How could I claim to love my son if I had no time to toss the baseball with him in the backyard? How could I honestly sing that silly love song I had composed for my daughter if I had no time to attend her track meets? And why should my wife believe my affections if I was too busy to sip lemonade with her on the back porch as the sun set?

Those backyard baseball drills, trips to the track meets, and back porch conversations at sunset spoke more eloquently about my love for my family than anything I said. *Agape* love costs; in these cases I paid only a little time and energy and received a lot of pleasure in return. But love can cost much more: sleepless hours by a hospital bed, painful sessions in the principal's office, agonizing trips to the drug rehab center, thousands of dollars for life's necessities, sleepless nights of worry and frustration, long days of listening and weeping. Real love is willing to pay almost any price for another's benefit.

Those two problems—being hard of hearing and struggling to walk—can prevent us from loving others. If we don't have ears to hear that commandment anymore, and if we never move beyond *knowing* to *doing*, we'll fail to obey the Great Commandment. John wanted his readers to understand that before he moved to his next topic: taking aim at some false teachers who were denying the humanity of Christ.

Drawing the Line (vv. 7-11)

The change in tone between verses 6 and 7 could hardly be more dramatic. In verse 6, John has just concluded his brief treatise on walking in love. If we're expecting him to continue down that path, we're in for a shock: "Many deceivers have gone out into the world, those who do not confess that Jesus Christ has come in the flesh; any such person is the deceiver and the antichrist!" (v. 7).

Then he proceeds to say that anyone who doesn't speak the truth about Christ doesn't know God. Furthermore, he tells his readers not to welcome any of these teachers into their homes or to greet them in any way, lest they partic-ipate in the evil deeds of these men. So much for John's treatise on "What the World Needs Now Is Love"!

To understand what is going on here, we need to know that there were three different kinds of ministries in the early church:

- There were the *apostles*, who had walked and talked with Jesus and been witnesses to the cross and resurrection. They were the undisputed leaders of the church and held in high esteem by all.
- There were the *prophets*, who were not attached to any church but wandered from church to church preaching and teaching. They were in a similar position as modern-day evangelists and were also held in high esteem. The prophets were seen as having special gifts from God and depended on the hospitality of the churches as they performed their itinerant ministries.
- Finally, there were the *elders*, who ministered and served within a local congregation. When Paul and Barnabas made their first missionary journey, one of their primary tasks was to ordain elders in all the churches they founded (Acts 14:23). The elders were the backbone of the early churches and the equivalent of our modern-day pastors.

What seems to have prompted John's stern warning in this passage concerns the work of some of the traveling prophets who were on their way to the church he was writing. Here's how William Barclay explains it:

> The wandering prophets did present a problem. Their position was one which was particularly liable to abuse. They had an enormous prestige; and it was possible for the most undesirable characters to enter into a way of life in which they moved from place to place, living in very considerable comfort at the expense of the local congregations. A clever rogue could make a very comfortable living as an itinerant prophet. . . . There is no doubt that in the early church these wandering prophets became a problem. Some of them were heretical teachers, even if they were sincerely convinced of their own teaching. Some were nothing better than plausible rogues who had found an easy way to make a comfortable living.[2]

Perhaps we can put this situation into a modern context. Imagine that an evangelist, holding revivals, is making the rounds of evangelical churches. He is bold, brash, and colorful and attracts big crowds everywhere he goes. For that reason, his calendar is full, and churches are clamoring to book him for a crusade.

But when he comes to your church, you notice some unsettling things about him. He is certainly bold, brash, and colorful, but his theology is suspect and his methods are coercive and manipulative. He uses a lot of fear and arm-twisting in his sermons, and, by the time the week is over, you're very glad to see him go. You wonder if the decisions made that week will stand the test of time.

It's possible that, the more you think about it, the more agitated you become. Is this man really preaching the Jesus of the Gospels? And is he using the methods Jesus used in his ministry? Do we really want people pledging allegiance to the Christ this man presented? You might even decide that this evangelist is doing more harm than good, that's he's preaching a false gospel. You eventually decide to be honest when people ask about him. For the sake of the truth and the gospel, you feel obligated to tell people to avoid him.

Something like that must have been at work in 2 John. John had seen and heard these wandering prophets and deemed them to be bad news. They were not only rogues, out to fleece good people, but also false teachers. They were espousing the gnostic idea that Jesus wasn't truly human, and John couldn't tolerate it. He wrote 2 John 7-11 to be as truthful as he could.

Still, we might wonder about the severity of his words. Don't even welcome these men at all? Have nothing to do with them? Isn't this a denial of the very teaching he's just given, that we love one another? Before we accuse John of not practicing what he has just preached, we need to consider two truths that might explain his extreme reaction to these teachers.

First, *the church was in a critical time in its history.* Though 2 John was written at the end of the first century, everything was still up for grabs theologically. The early church was still trying to figure out what it believed and who Jesus was. The gnostics were a legitimate threat, and John and others wanted to make sure that their denial of the humanity of Christ was refuted. The incarnation was crucial to the gospel story, and John didn't want the gnostics to get a firm foothold. So, he spoke boldly and decisively.

Second, *John himself had experienced the humanity of Jesus and couldn't bear the thought that people would deny it.* Think of it: John had walked and talked with Jesus, heard him laugh and cry, seen the way he loved outcasts and sinners, fished with him on the Sea of Galilee, and conversed with him after the resurrection. He *knew* Jesus was a real human being and was incredulous that anyone would say otherwise.

When it came to these wandering preachers flippantly saying Jesus wasn't really a human being, he drew a line: "Everyone who does not abide in the teaching of Christ, but goes beyond it, does not have God; whoever abides in the teaching has both the Father and the Son" (v. 9). Some truths are worth fighting for, and, for John, the truth about Jesus' humanity was one of them.

A Comma, Not a Period (vv. 12-13)

John concludes 2 John by saying he plans to "come to you and talk with you face to face, so that our joy may be complete" (v. 12b). There's nothing like face-to-face conversation. Paper and ink—and email, instant messages, and tweets—are not the same as talking personally to someone. John plans to continue this discussion at some time in the future. In the meantime, he sends greetings from another church—"The children of your elect sister send you their greetings" (v. 13)—and signs off. His letter was brief enough to fit on one sheet of papyrus, which would have made it easy to send and circulate.

He has used this one-page tract to say two important things: (1) love is the essence of the Christian Way, and (2) some truths, like who Jesus was, are worth fighting for. *Love* and *truth*. Those two words capture the heart of John's message in 2 John.

BAD LEADERSHIP (3 JOHN)

Third John addresses a second problem in the early church: bad leadership. John mentions three men in the letter: (1) Gaius, the recipient of the letter and a man John knows and loves; (2) Diotrephes, a man John knows but also distrusts and criticizes; and (3) Demetrius, a man John commends to Gaius and his church as a dependable leader.

These three men are the main characters in 3 John, and what John says to and about them gives us a crash course on church leadership. Let's look at these three men and what they teach us.

Gaius: Mr. Hospitality (vv. 1-8)

Third John is addressed to a man named Gaius, who must have been the pastor or lay leader of a first-century church. John begins the letter by writing of his love for the man: "The elder, to the beloved Gaius, whom I love in the truth"

(v. 1). John then mentions two reasons he feels such a kinship with Gaius—Gaius continues to walk in the truth, and Gaius is practicing Christian hospitality.

The situation in 3 John is the opposite of the situation in 2 John. In 2 John, John was leery of a group of prophets who roamed from church to church preaching the gospel. He saw those traveling evangelists as both unscrupulous and doctrinally dangerous. He wrote 2 John to address this situation and to tell the members of that church to avoid these false teachers at all costs.

But in 3 John, John writes to commend a different group of prophets to this church and to thank Gaius and his cohorts for showing hospitality to them in the past. Some of those traveling preachers must have reported to John about the kind treatment they had received from the church: "I was overjoyed when some of the friends arrived and testified to your faithfulness to the truth, namely how you walk in the truth" (v. 3). Later he adds, ". . . they have testified to your love before the church" (v. 6).

John wants Gaius and his fellow church members to continue this hospitality to the visiting prophets: "You will do well to send them on in a manner worthy of God, for they began their journey for the sake of Christ, accepting no support from nonbelievers. Therefore, we ought to support such people, so that we may become co-workers with the truth" (vv. 6-8). Gaius and his church had been hospitable in the past, and John wanted to make sure they would continue to be hospitable in the future.

In *The Letters of John*, William Hendricks reminds us that, in the ancient world, hospitality was more than just being nice; it was an essential service travelers depended on:

> Hospitality in the ancient world was no small item. A traveling generation such as ours, glazed-eyed from the neon signs of competing motels, is scarcely able to appreciate what the hotel business was like in the ancient world. If a traveler was to have shelter on a journey, he was dependent on the hospitality of friends and strangers. Nor was this ancient hospitality just a casual provision of a night's lodging. As can be seen in 2 John 10-11, the host involved himself with the guests and was commonly associated in the guests' actions and teachings.[3]

It's no wonder John found Gaius so commendable. He had proven to be Mr. Hospitality, a gracious and welcoming host who had enhanced the ministries of the traveling preachers.

Diotrephes: Mr. Intimidator (vv. 9-10)

The second character mentioned in 3 John was anything *but* Mr. Hospitality. He was, in fact, Mr. Inhospitable or Mr. Intimidator. His name was Diotrephes, and he must have been a member of the same church as Gaius. Diotrephes had an authoritarian leadership style that was divisive and contentious. Even the brief description John gives of him in verses 9-10 tells us much about him:

The Truth

The "truth" includes (1) something you know (2 John 1), (2) walk in (2 John 2; 3 John 3, 4), (3) abide in as a believer forever (2 John 2). This Christian truth, furthermore, (4) finds definition in the commandments (1 John 3:23). Believers are (5) challenged to become coworkers with truth (3 John 8).

- *He had an ego problem.* John writes, "Diotrephes, who likes to put himself first, does not acknowledge our authority" (v. 9b). The phrase "who likes to put himself first" says it all.
- *He was authoritarian.* He wouldn't recognize John's authority. He also wouldn't welcome the visiting prophets, and if anyone in the church did welcome them, he would try to get them expelled from the church. Diotrephes wanted to be "the man in charge."
- *He was critical of others.* He was not only "spreading false charges" about John but also must have been criticizing "the friends" who were coming to minister among them and those who welcomed these guests. Diotrephes was mad at everyone.
- *He was inhospitable and unfriendly.* Diotrephes was the opposite of Gaius, who befriended the visiting guests and even supported them financially. Diotrephes was, to put it plainly, a pain in the neck. He wasn't the kind of person you would invite to your house for dinner. He was the kind of person with a knack for alienating people and stirring up trouble.

Put those four characteristics together and you have a leadership style that has been evident since humans first appeared on earth. It's the Diotrephes-Domination School of Leadership, and its rules have been the same in every generation:

(1) Lead by intimidation; (2) Have strict rules and enforce them vigorously; (3) Don't tolerate dissent or even suggestion; (4) Make fear your primary motivator.

Those rules define a leadership style still evident today. Sometimes it is even called "strong leadership." Classrooms, offices, sports teams, families, and churches are often led by people using this style of leadership. Sometimes systems and institutions thrive numerically and financially under these kinds of leaders. But no one in any of these systems or institutions is having a very good time. So-called "strong leaders" might produce results, but they never produce joy.

Demetrius: Mr. Dependable (vv. 11-12)

The final character John mentions in 3 John is Demetrius, who may have been either the leader of the visiting prophets or a member of the same church as Gaius and Diotrephes. Whichever he was, he had opted for a different leadership style from Diotrephes. John presents just a brief glimpse of Demetrius in verses 11-12, but it is enough for us to conclude three things about him:

- *He was a good, dependable person.* Before mentioning Demetrius, John writes, "Beloved, do not imitate what is evil but imitate what is good. Whoever does good is from God; whoever does evil has not seen God" (v. 11). The insinuation was clear: Demetrius was good and from God, but Diotrephes? Well, you get the point. Demetrius was the good man, the one to be imitated.
- *He had the support of the group.* John comments that "everyone has testified favorably about Demetrius" (v. 12a). Leadership is always a two-way street, and Demetrius was already halfway there. He didn't have to win the respect of the church; he already had it.
- *He was a person of truth.* Demetrius was even supported by "the truth itself" (v. 12b). He wasn't held in high esteem only by the people; even truth applauded him. And so did John.

Put those three characteristics together and you get the Demetrius-Submission School of Leadership. It too has always been governed by a certain set of rules: (1) Trust the group; (2) Motivate through encouragement; (3) Look for the best in others; (4) Try to create a laughter-filled environment where people enjoy themselves. In this school of leadership, the people being led produce remarkable results and have a good time doing it.

When we read 3 John we can almost feel the tension in it. Visiting prophets were probably on the way to this church. Some in the church wanted to welcome them and show them Christian hospitality. Some in the church wanted to shun them and have nothing to do with them. John sided with the first group. He believed these visiting evangelists were legitimate teachers, worthy of love and support, so he wrote 3 John to weigh in on the debate.

But there was an even bigger issue at stake in this church. The church was debating the question, "What kind of church are we going to be?" Are we going to be a Diotrephes kind of church—heavy on rules, regulations, accountability, and criticism? Or are we going to be a Demetrius kind of church—heavy on hospitality, freedom, trust, and grace? Are we going to be a *domination* kind of church or a *submission* kind of church?

The person on the hot seat in 3 John was Gaius. Since the letter was addressed specifically to him, it seems that John assumed him to be the leader who would sway the church one way or the other. But now that 3 John has brought the subject to the surface, we know that *we* are on the hot seat, too. We must decide what kind of leadership we want in our church and what kind of church ours will be. Do we want Diotrephes or Demetrius as our pastor? Which of those two leadership styles do we want our deacons and committees to choose?

The decision about leadership extends beyond the church, too. We must decide what kind of leader we will be in our families, jobs, sports teams, and other groups. Third John brings our own relational style to our attention and reminds us that our options are simple: Diotrephes or Demetrius? Domination or submission? Rigidity or freedom? The choices we make will determine not only our own happiness but also, to a great extent, the happiness of the people we lead.

Final Greetings (vv. 13-15)

The final greeting in 3 John is almost identical to the one in 2 John. John concludes by writing that he has much more he would like to say but would rather not have to use pen and ink to say it. He hopes to see them soon so they can talk face to face. Then he sends greetings from "the friends," those who travel and minister in the name of Christ, and asks the church members to greet the "the friends there, each by name" (v. 15).

The similar closings of 2 and 3 John suggest that the same author wrote both letters. The apostle John, or one of his close disciples, desired to make sure the early church kept its bearings and its passion. In 2 John, he wanted the church to be discerning and not fall for false teaching. In 3 John, he wanted the church to be discerning and not fall for false leadership. In both letters, he wanted those early Christians to know and live the truth.

BAD LIVING (JUDE)

There were two at least subgroups among the gnostics in the late first-century world. There were the *ascetics*, who, believed that the body is evil and tried to subdue and punish it. And there were the *antinomians*, who gave themselves permission to do anything they wanted to do. Since the body was evil and didn't really matter, the antinomians reasoned, why not give in to its every desire? The letter of Jude is addressed to this second group, antinomian gnostics in the church who were using the doctrine of grace to justify immoral living.

> **"The Consequences of Putting Yourself First"**
>
> 3 John may continue to serve . . . as both a call for cooperative efforts and a reminder of the dissension which so often strikes churches when harsh measures are taken to exclude certain beliefs, when communication between individuals and churches is broken, or when church leaders allow personal ambitions to influence their actions.
>
> R. Alan Culpepper, *1 John, 2 John, 3 John* (Atlanta: John Knox Press, 1985), 135.

One unusual fact about Jude is that it is repeated, almost verbatim, in the book of 2 Peter. Either the writer of 2 Peter borrowed liberally from Jude, Jude borrowed liberally from him, or both used a common source when they penned their letters. One thing is certain: both letters address the same situation. They both speak against antinomian Gnosticism and the bad living it was producing in the early church.

A Beginning to Remember (vv. 1-2)

The writer of Jude—probably Judas, the brother of Jesus—begins his letter with a bang. He identifies himself as "a servant of Jesus Christ and brother of James" (v. 1a). Perhaps out of a sense of modesty and humility, Jude refuses to identify himself as the brother of Jesus, preferring instead to call himself simply a servant of Jesus Christ. He then identifies his recipients as "those who are called, who are beloved in God the Father, and kept safe for Jesus Christ" (v. 1b). The three attributes in that description of his recipients are worth noting—and holding on to:

- *Called.* This one word is a reminder to us all that God took the initiative in our relationship with him. Incredibly, God pursued and called us. Francis Thompson's poem about the "Hound of Heaven" describes his spiritual journey. Through all the ups and downs and ins and outs of his life, Thompson found that the Hound of Heaven kept pursuing him. It wasn't that he found God; it was, instead, that God found him—and kept finding him. Of all the titles that shape and motivate us, there is none more significant or powerful than this one: "called of God."
- *Beloved.* When Jesus was baptized, he heard a voice saying to him, "You are my Son, the Beloved; with you I am well pleased" (Lk 3:22b). Like Jesus, we all get to hear those words if we listen closely enough. More than twenty years ago, Henri Nouwen wrote a book titled *Life of the Beloved* and concluded it with these words: "As those who are chosen, blessed, broken, and given, we are called to live our lives with a deep inner joy and peace. It is the life of the Beloved, lived in a world constantly trying to convince us that the burden is on us to prove that we are worth of being loved."[4] Jude reminds his readers in the introduction of his letter that they are the beloved of God.
- *Kept Safe.* This phrase is reminiscent of 1 Peter 2:25 where Peter refers to Christ as "the shepherd and guardian of your souls." We are kept safe *for* Jesus Christ, but we are also kept safe *by* Jesus Christ. Because of him, our relationship with God is safe and secure. Our shepherd and guardian will even die—no, has already died—to make sure we make it home safely.

Having assured his readers that they possess those three qualities, Jude then proceeds to wish them mercy, peace, and love in abundance. They are dealing with some heavy issues, but they have more than enough resources to stand firm in the truth.

Contending for the Faith (vv. 3-4)

Jude had intended to write a different kind of letter, a letter about "the salvation we share" (v. 3a), but that letter would have to wait for another time. Recent events in the church had convinced him that he had to address "the elephant in the room"—those who claimed to follow Christ but who had turned the gospel of grace into the gospel of "if-it-feels-good-do-it." He needed to stress to his readers the importance of contending "for the faith that was once for all entrusted to the saints" (v. 3b).

These intruders have become part of the church, but Jude has nothing kind to say about them. He mentions three things about them: (1) they've already been designated for the condemnation reserved for the ungodly; (2) they pervert the grace of God into licentiousness; and (3) they deny the Lord and Master, Jesus Christ. In Jude's mind, these intruders have those three strikes against them and shouldn't have any credibility in the church.

It was bad enough that these antinomian gnostics were teaching false things, but it was even worse that they were living such brazenly immoral lives. Heresy is awful, but immorality and debauchery are simply not allowed among people who know and love Jesus Christ. Christians are called, beloved, and kept safe and know how high the bar has been set; they cannot stand for some of their fellow believers to trample on the grace of God or to ignore the plain teachings of their Lord.

Jude not only wanted to contend for the faith himself but also wanted

Beloved

AΩ The KJV reads "sanctified," but modern translations have "beloved." Since believers are both *sanctified* by God and *beloved* by God, either reading would suffice. To *sanctify* means "to make holy," i.e., "separate." Paul wrote about the Corinthian Christians, some of whom had been egregious sinners, "But you were washed, but you were sanctified, but you were justified in the name of the Lord Jesus and in the Spirit of our God" (1 Cor 6:11). Christians abide in God's love that is multiplied (Jude 2). They are told, "Keep yourselves in the love of God" (Jude 21). "Beloved" carries the meaning of people loved by God and also by the writer. It is a term of special endearment used to refer to those who are close to and have a special relationship with God. The word carries the meaning of someone who cares deeply for another. Using the title "beloved" underscores the importance of what the writer is about to say in his letter. The word says, "The message that follows comes from my heart and shows my concern for you. It is a message of great importance."

his readers to contend for the faith. He wanted them to remember their calling as followers of Christ and to stand firm against those who would sully the gospel.

The Lessons of History (vv. 5-7)

To underscore the judgment awaiting these false teachers and immoral intruders, Jude mentions three lessons from history that he wants the people to remember. All three are examples of those who failed to trust God and live for God—and suffered terribly as a result. He reminds his readers of the fate of Israel, the fate of the angels, and the fate of Sodom and Gomorrah.

- *The fate of Israel.* Jude refers to Numbers 13 and 14 where God had led the people of Israel to the brink of the promised land only to see them shrink back in fear. The people chose to believe the ten spies who said they couldn't conquer the land of Canaan and decided not to try. God was so incensed at their lack of faith that he decreed that, with the exception of Joshua and Caleb, who did believe they could take the promised land, all the Israelites over the age of twenty would never see Canaan. Their faithlessness was their downfall.
- *The fate of the angels.* In verse 6, Jude refers to the *Book of Enoch*, which seems to have been behind much of his thinking. The *Book of Enoch* had much to say about fallen angels—angels stripped of their glory because of pride or lust. While this reference is unfamiliar to most of us, it probably wasn't unfamiliar to Jude's original readers. They knew about the fallen angels in *Enoch*, and they knew Jude was saying that the antinomians, because of their own pride and lust, would fall as well.
- *The fate of Sodom and Gomorrah.* No incident in Jewish history made more of an impression on the Jewish people than the sin of Sodom and Gomorrah. Because of their wickedness, the cities of Sodom and Gomorrah were destroyed by the fire of God (see Gen 19:1-11). That event is mentioned in Deuteronomy, Amos, Isaiah, Jeremiah, Zephaniah, Lamentations, Ezekiel, Matthew, Luke, Romans, 2 Peter, and Revelation. Now Jude joins the chorus and says the antinomians are in the lineage of Sodom and Gomorrah and destined to receive the judgment of God.

The Israelites in Numbers, the angels in the *Book of Enoch*, and the cities of Sodom and Gomorrah in Genesis all felt God's wrath because of their sin. In Jude's mind, it was now the antinomians' turn to experience that wrath.

Contempt for the Holy (vv. 8-10)

These verses are difficult to comprehend because they refer to a story about angels that is foreign to us. They also quote an apocryphal book *The Assumption of Moses*, which is foreign to us as well. If the story of the archangel Michael doesn't seem familiar to you, don't feel bad. It's from that apocryphal book and not from the Bible. Jude's fondness for quoting nonbiblical sources makes the letter seem strange to us—and also delayed Jude's entry into the canon of Scripture.

The point of these verses is that the antinomians had lost their sense of the holy. In fact, they had developed an outright contempt for the holy. Go back to those fish in Mammoth Cave I mentioned earlier in this study that have become so accustomed to the darkness that they can no longer see the light.

Sodom and Gomorrah

Sodom and Gomorrah were two of a group of five towns, the Pentapolis: Sodom, Gomorrah, Admah, Zeboim, and Bela. The Pentapolis region is also collectively referred to as "the Cities of the Plain" (Gen 13:12) since they were all sited on the plain of the River Jordan, in an area that constituted the southern limit of the lands of the Canaanites (Gen 10:19). Lot, a nephew of Abram (Abraham). chose to live in Sodom because of the proximity of good grazing for his flocks (Gen 13:5-11).

In Genesis 18, God sends three angels who appear as men to Abraham in the plains of Mamre. God reveals to Abraham that he will investigate Sodom and Gomorrah, because their cry is great, "and because their sin is very grievous" (vv. 20-21). In response, Abraham reverently inquires of God if he would spare the city if 50 righteous people were found in it, then 45, then 30, then 20, or even 10, with God affirming he would not destroy it after each request, for the sake of the righteous yet dwelling therein.

The two angels of God proceed to Sodom and are met by Abraham's righteous nephew Lot, who extends hospitality of his home to them. Genesis 19:4-5 describes what followed: "But before they lay down, the men of the city, the men of Sodom, both young and old, all the people to the last man, surrounded the house; and they called to Lot, 'Where are the men who came to you tonight? Bring them out to us, that we may know them'" (NIV: "can have sex with them"; NJB: "can have intercourse with them").

In response, Lot refuses to give his guests to the inhabitants of Sodom, and instead offers them his two virgin daughters to "do to them whatever you like" (Gen 19:8, NASB). However, the men of Sodom refuse this offer and threaten to do worse to Lot than they would have done to his guests.

Lot's angelic guests rescue him and strike the men with blindness. They then command Lot to gather his family and leave, revealing their intention to destroy Sodom and Gomorrah. As they make their escape, the angels command Lot and his family not to look back under any circumstance; however, Lot's wife ignores their warning and looks back longingly at the city and becomes a pillar of salt.

For the sins of their inhabitants, Sodom, Gomorrah, Admah, and Zeboim were destroyed by "brimstone and fire from the Lord out of heaven" (Gen 19:24-25). In Christianity and Islam, their names have become synonymous with impenitent sin and their fall with a proverbial manifestation of God's wrath. The term "Sodom" has been used as a metaphor for vice and sexual deviation. The story has given rise to words in several languages, including the English word "sodomy," a term used today predominantly in law (derived from traditional Christian usage) to describe non-vaginal intercourse as well as bestiality.

John Keating Wiles, "Sodom/Gommorah/Cities of the Plain," *Mercer Dictionary of the Bible* (ed. Watson E. Mills; Macon GA: Mercer University Press, 1990) 839–40.

The darkness has become their natural habitat. It's possible to become so accustomed to darkness that we're no longer able to detect the holy. Nothing is sacred anymore.

Jude puts it this way: "But these people slander whatever they do not understand, and they are destroyed by those things that, like irrational animals, they know by instinct" (v. 10). In other words, "these people" were flying upside down—and didn't even know it. And, like those angels in *The Assumption of Moses*, they were destined to fall.

More Lessons from History and Nature (vv. 11-16)

Just to make sure his readers fully grasp the evil of these intruders and the coming wrath awaiting them, Jude mentions several other examples of people who had disobeyed God—and paid the price for it. He quickly cites a trio of evildoers:

• Cain, the first murderer in the Bible.
• Balaam, who in Numbers 22–25 is cast as the character who taught Israel how to sin.
• Korah, who in Numbers 16 rebels against the guidance of Moses and dies because of it.

Then Jude shifts to examples from nature to describe the lives and fate of these evil intruders:

• They're like waterless clouds, carried along by the winds.
• They're like autumn trees, without fruit, twice dead, uprooted.
• They're like wild waves of the sea, casting up the foam of their own shame.
• They're like wandering stars, for whom the deepest darkness has been reserved forever.

He wraps up his case against these antinomians by once again quoting the *Book of Enoch*. It was these antinomian intruders Enoch had in mind when he prophesied, "See, the Lord is coming with ten thousands of his holy ones, to execute judgment on all, and to convict everyone of all the deeds of ungodliness that they have committed in such an ungodly way, and of all the harsh things that ungodly sinners have spoken against him" (Enoch 1:9).

These antinomians, Jude concludes, are heretics, grumblers, malcontents, lustful, bombastic, and flattering when they need to be. He has obviously looked long and hard and can't find one thing in their lives that deserves praise. Jude joins Enoch in castigating these intruders and predicting their imminent demise.

The Antidote (vv. 17-23)

Most of Jude's letter is a diatribe against these antinomian Christians and what he perceived to be their betrayal of the true gospel of grace. Verses 3-16 are devoted to the danger presented by these unscrupulous people, so most of the letter is negative and critical in tone. But, at the end of the letter, Jude gives some specific ways his readers can take a stand against this movement that threatened to destroy the church.

His antidote for the evil being spread among them contained five specific directives.

- *Remember.* They were to remember that this situation had been predicted by the apostles themselves. The apostles had warned them of scoffers who delighted in indulging their own ungodly lusts, so they shouldn't be particularly surprised or dismayed by these intruders.
- *Build yourselves up.* Jude tells them to "build yourselves up in your most holy faith" (v. 20a). They were to guard their personal faith and encourage one another to learn and live the truth.
- *Keep yourselves in the love of God.* In a divisive situation such as the one they were facing, these early Christians needed to anchor their lives in God's love. It would have been easy to sink into bitterness, anger, depression, cynicism, or any other negative states. They needed to focus on God's love and keep receiving that love and giving it to others.
- *Look forward to the mercy.* That line is great and one worth remembering. As we face the future, not sure exactly what will befall us, we can be steadied by the assurance that "the mercy of our Lord Jesus Christ" awaits us. We are held in the grace and mercy of God.
- *Have mercy.* Jude's final admonition concerns people in the early church who were falling prey to the false gospel of the antinomians. To those who were wavering, he says to show mercy. To those who were leaning toward the false gospel, "snatch them out of the fire" (v. 23a). And to those who had already

cast their lot with the heretics, "have mercy on still others with fear, hating even the tunic defiled by their bodies" (v. 23b).

It is always true that the best antidote for bad Christianity is good Christianity. One devout life, lived truthfully and gracefully before others, is the best antidote for false faith. Jude knew that, and we know it, too. If we can remember that falsehood and division are part of religious life, that we are to focus on building our own faith and the faith of others, that we are to keep our lives and our focus on the love of God, that we are to lean into the mercy of a gracious Lord, and that we are to have mercy on those who stumble and fall, we'll be part of the antidote instead of the disease.

A Closing to Remember (vv. 24-25)

Three times in the New Testament, God is described as "the God who is able." In Romans 16:25, Paul praises the God who is able to give us strength. In Ephesians 3:20, Paul describes a God who is able to do more than we can think or dream. And here in Jude, Jude closes his letter by praising a God who is able to do three things: keep us from falling, make us stand without blemish before God, and escort us triumphantly into the presence of God's glory.

Jude ends his letter with this ascription of praise: "To the only God our Savior, through Jesus Christ our Lord, be glory, majesty, power, and authority, before all time and now and forever. Amen" (v. 25).

Conclusion

We might admit that the letter of Jude may never become one of our favorite books in the Bible. It is filled with strange references and allusions, it seems negative and critical, and, though it mentions and advocates grace, it seems to be a bit short on grace itself. In my long years as a pastor, I'm not sure I ever preached a sermon from Jude.

But let's consider the one thing Jude does for us: it makes us consider the place of truth in our lives. Jude believed he had found a wonderful, life-changing, nonnegotiable truth in Jesus Christ. It was a truth worth fighting for, and, obviously, Jude was ready to do that.

In *No Place for Truth*, David Wells writes,

The apostles asserted that Christ alone is the truth in the midst of a world that was more religiously diverse than any we have known in the West until relatively recently. We today are far closer in religious temper to apostolic times than any period since the Reformation. . . .

Admittedly, the apostolic world was small and ours is not. Theirs, however, was a cauldron of conflicting religious claims within which the Christian movement would have remained tiny if not for one fact: the first Christians knew their faith was absolutely true, that it could brook no rivals, and so they sought no compromises. That was the kind of integrity that God, the Holy Spirit, blessed and used in the ancient world in spreading the knowledge of Christ. We today are not so commonly persuaded or, I dare say, so commonly blessed.[5]

All four of the letters we have examined in this study bear that unmistakable mark. They all assume that their faith is absolutely true, that it can brook no rivals, and so they seek no compromises. John refuses to compromise with the gnostics in 1 and 2 John, and he refuses to compromise with bullying leaders in 3 John. Jude refuses to compromise with the antinomians, no matter how superior and advanced they claim to be. Both John and Jude are adamant and passionate about the truth they have found in Christ.

If nothing else, our study of these letters has probably nudged us to consider our own truth. What

Falling

AΩ The term translated "falling" is a word that means "slipping," as used of both of a surefooted horse that does not stumble and of a person who is a good and thus does not fall into error. The psalmist has written of God's loving care: "He will not let your foot slip" (Ps 121:3, NIV). To walk with God is to walk in safety even on the most dangerous and the most slippery path. When mountaineers tackle a daring climb, they rope themselves together so that if one climber slips, the others take the weight and no one falls. The author calls us to bind ourselves to God who will "keep us from falling."

truth motivates our lives? What truth do we consider indispensable to our faith? What truth so moves us that we are adamant and passionate about it?

I once heard someone described as "having his feet planted firmly in midair." Could that be me? Could that be you? One thing we now know for certain: it could not be either John or Jude.

QUESTIONS FOR REFLECTION AND DISCUSSION

1. Do you agree that religion has often been linked directly to the worst examples of human behavior? How has the church blessed you? And how has it caused you grief?
2. Second John is about bad teaching. What do you consider to be the most glaring example of bad teaching in contemporary Christianity?
3. Third John is about bad leadership. How would you rate the leadership in today's church? Which of the two schools of leadership mentioned in 3 John do you think is more effective in our day?
4. Jude is about bad living. Are there any antinomians in our day—people who abuse grace? What do you think Jude says to people today? Is Jude's letter helpful or overly judgmental?
5. What do you think of the absolute truth claims of John and Jude? How can we be tolerant of others and not have our feet planted firmly in midair?
6. What are the essential ingredients in your Christian faith, the indispensable truths that you have built your life on?

SUGGESTIONS FOR WORSHIP AND PREACHING

An Order of Worship

This final worship service is built around the inspiring introduction to the book of Jude. Though Jude is primarily focused on warning the early Christians about the antinomians, who used grace to justify immoral behavior, the initial greeting in the letter is a glorious reminder of our true identity in Christ.

The Worship of God
"To those who are called, who are beloved in God the Father, and kept safe for Jesus Christ . . . ." (Jude 1)

Spoken Call to Worship
The Chiming of the Hour
Hymn: "The Church's One Foundation"
Choral Meditation: "Spirit of the Living God" (Words and Music: Daniel Iverson, copyright 1935, 1963 by Moody Bible Institute)

Invocation

Hymn: "Tell It Out with Gladness"

Receiving of Tithes and Offerings

The Singing of the Doxology

Offertory Prayer

The Word of the Lord: Jude 1-3

    Leader: This is the word of the Lord.

    Congregation: Thanks be to God.

Choral Reflection: "Let Your Light Shine" (Craig Courtney, copyright 1993 by Beckenhorst Press, 1993)

Sermon: "Spiritual Amnesia"

Hymn of Response: "Living for Jesus"

Spoken Benediction

    Leader: Thank you, God, for calling us,

    Congregation: For telling us that we are your beloved children,

    Leader: And for keeping us safe in Jesus Christ.

    All: Use us this week to make a difference for you in the world, Amen.

Postlude

A SERMON SKETCH: "SPIRITUAL AMNESIA" (JUDE 1-3)

Introduction

This may be the first sermon you've ever heard from the little letter of Jude. That's because the letter is a scalding condemnation of some people in the early church who were known as the "antinomians." The antinomians used the doctrine of grace to allow themselves to do anything they wanted to do, and Jude took them to task for their perversion of the gospel. His letter was a stinging diatribe against those who abused grace, and, since diatribes are not very edifying, we tend to avoid Jude in favor of more positive biblical fare.

But Jude begins his letter with one of the finer greetings in the entire New Testament. Before he ever writes a negative word about the antinomians, he reminds his reader of their true identity in Christ. Since spiritual amnesia is as prevalent today as it was when Jude wrote his letter at the end of the first century, this greeting can remind us, too, of who we are in Christ.

Called

Jude addresses his letter "to those who are called." That one word, "called," reminds us that God took the initiative, sought us out, and gave us a mission. Few of us get a dramatic, Damascus Road kind of call, but we still sense that God is beckoning us to follow and serve him. We can't prove our call—and much of the world would deem us delusional if we proclaimed it too loudly—but we still believe it to be true. We are called by God to serve him in specific ways.

Beloved

Jude continues his greeting by reminding his readers that they are "beloved in God the Father." That's an echo of the blessing Jesus received at baptism. There must have been times in his ministry—when the Pharisees made his life miserable, when his disciples had no clue who he was or what he came to do, or when he faced the horrors of the cross—that Jesus clung to the promise as if his life depended on it. He needed to remember that he was beloved by God, and so do we. Remembering that we are both *called* and *beloved* by God can see us through many a dark day.

Kept Safe

Jude also reminded his readers that they were "kept safe." Some translations say "kept safe *for* Jesus Christ," implying the hope that they would one day be in his presence. Some translations say "kept safe *by* Jesus Christ," implying that Jesus himself is the reason they can approach God with confidence. Either way, those early Christians did not need to wonder about their salvation or worry about their standing with God. They were safe and could live with joyful hope.

Conclusion

The Christians in the first century were constantly facing identity crises. The world at large did not understand them and saw them as deluded members of a strange cult. It would have been easy, in that kind of environment, for them to give up and try to become more "respectable." That is why church leaders like Peter, Paul, John, and Jude kept reminding them of their real identity. They were the people of God, children of a loving Father, a royal nation, a holy priesthood, and so forth. They didn't need to give up or grow discouraged; they needed to claim their true identity and live with confidence. The New

Testament writers consistently kept bolstering the self-image of those early Christians.

We face the same dilemma in our day. We Christians seem to be becoming more and more marginalized in our culture. It's easy in our world to hide our beliefs or fear for our reputation. And then we read this old greeting in Jude and take heart. We are called, beloved, and kept safe. Secure in that identity, we will live with joyful hope—even if we seem like fools to the outside world.

NOTES

1. Charles Kimball, *When Religion Becomes Evil* (San Francisco: Harper & Row, 2002) 1.

2. William Barclay, *The Letters of John and Jude* (Louisville: Westminster John Knox Press, 1976) 133.

3. William Hendricks, *The Letters of John* (Nashville: Convention Press, 1970) 35.

4. Henri Nouwen, *Life of the Beloved* (New York: Crossroad, 1996) 103.

5. David Wells, *No Place for Truth* (Grand Rapids: Eerdmans, 1993) 104.

TEACHING
1, 2, 3 JOHN AND
JUDE TO YOUTH

This study of 1, 2, 3 John and Jude can be especially appropriate for youth, who are in the process of deciding what is true for them and what they will choose to build their lives around. Certainly, youth today are struggling with what to believe and what deserves their best energy and allegiance. These four letters in the New Testament can be a great resource for helping them learn and live the truth. As a youth minister or youth teacher, you will find in 1, 2, 3 John and Jude some material that can energize youth and encourage them in their faith journey.

It will be important that you, as the leader of the study, read the teacher's guide and know the background material for each session. Each of the four sessions is based on a focal passage in one of the letters, but beyond the focal passage is a wealth of material that needs to be understood and explained.

The question that gives shape to the study is *How can I learn and live the truth?* Each of the four sessions will offer part of an answer to that question.

The first session, built around 1 John 1:5-10, is titled "Loving God: The Games Christians Play." In this passage, John mentions two games Christians play—charades and a game we're calling denial—and calls his readers to quit playing those games and to get honest with God. Much of 1 John focuses on the truth about loving God, and this session with the youth will give them an opportunity to look honestly at their relationship with God and to stop playing religious games.

The second session, built around 1 John 3:11-24, is titled "Loving People: Getting Personal." This session leads youth to think about loving the people in their lives and to express that love in personal and tangible ways. John has much to say about what love looks like, and this session will enable the youth to ponder what he has to say and begin to put those truths into their own lives.

The third session, built around 1 John 5:18-21, is titled "Following Jesus: Getting a New Life Map." Youth know that Christians are supposed to be different, but this session will show them *how* Christians are different. As they study these verses about the new truth Christ gives a person, they will have the opportunity to decide if they are willing to follow Christ down a narrow road.

The fourth session, built around the little letter of 3 John, is titled "Learning to Lead: Who's in Charge Here?" This final session will focus on the issue of leadership. Third John addresses a leadership problem in the early church and lays out two distinct leadership styles. In this session, the youth will have a chance to think about the people who lead them and also to think about their own style of leadership.

By the time you finish the four sessions of this study, the youth should be much better acquainted with some books in the Bible that are probably unfamiliar to them. Beyond that, they should also have a better understanding of essential Christian truth—what that truth is and how it affects their lives.

Some sessions include a list of materials to use as object lessons, and I recommend having several Bibles on hand. If you desire, the students can use their phones to look up Scripture. Biblegateway.com is a great website that offers Scripture in a wide variety of translations. Finally, be sure to have pens or pencils and paper available—or a dry-erase board with markers.

Study Outline
Session 1: Loving God: The Games Christians Play (1 John 1:5-10)
Session 2: Loving People: Getting Personal (1 John 3:11-24)
Session 3: Following Jesus: Getting a New Life Map (1 John 5:18-21)
Session 4: Learning to Lead: Who's in Charge Here? (3 John)

LOVING GOD: THE GAMES CHRISTIANS PLAY

Focal Text—1 John 1:5-10

Materials: Recording of the Joe South Song, "The Games People Play" (available on YouTube)

Learning Goal

This first session encourages youth to have an honest faith that refuses to play games with God or people. It examines two "games" John mentions in these verses and challenges the youth to avoid the games Christians often play.

Introducing the Session

1. As the youth gather, have playing in the background the old Joe South song, "The Games People Play." Begin the study by going over the words to that song, defining the idiom of "playing games with people" (manipulating, deceiving, or using strategies against others to gain something for yourself), and telling the youth that our verses from 1 John are about some of the games Christians play.

2. Ask the youth to describe some of the games they think Christians play. The question we want to consider in this session is *How can I build a faith in God that is honest and real?*

3. After reading the teacher's guide, give the youth a brief synopsis of 1 John: who wrote it, who he was writing to, and what his major themes are. Explain that the early Christians were struggling with doctrinal issues and disillusionment issues, and see if the youth think those issues are still a problem today.

Exploring the Text

1. Ask someone to read 1 John 1:5-10. You might ask the youth their initial reaction to those verses.

2. Reread verses 5-7 and introduce the game of charades to the youth. Explain that one person portrays an action without using words, and the rest of the group has to guess the action. You can even play the game for a while if you desire. Then tell them that a Christ follower named John wrote to believers in the early church who were playing their own version of this game. They were pretending to be Christian without living the Christian life. The goal in this game was to look Christian, to portray the image, without being changed on the inside. Point out that Jesus called the Pharisees "hypocrites," which literally means "one who wears a mask." In essence, Jesus said they were playing charades.

Discuss

• Talk together about examples of Christians playing charades today. Why might people do this?

• Invite students to share, if they are willing, about a time when they pretended to be Christians even though their life choices didn't reflect Christ. Why did they choose to act this way? What happened as a result? How could they make better choices next time?

• Ask whether anyone has known someone who claimed to be Christian but whose life didn't reflect Christ. If so, how did this person make them feel? How do they think we should react to such people?

3. Read verses 8-10 and explain that some early Christians were playing another game: the game of denial. When we play this game, we try to look holy and innocent and won't admit our sin. Use the teacher's guide to find illustrative material to describe this game. Talk about the difference between being holy and innocent and being sinful and forgiven. Stress to the youth that the gospel is about grace, not works. We can be honest with God because God doesn't demand perfection from us.

Discuss

• Talk together about examples of Christians playing the game of denial today. Why might people do this?

• Invite them to share, if they are willing, about a time when they viewed others as more sinful than they are. Why did they do this? Do they believe that God looks at varying "degrees" of sinfulness, or that God views us all as equal sinners? Why does this matter?

• Ask the group why it is important to admit that we are sinners in need of forgiveness—even if we think we make great, godly choices all the time.

Closing the Session

1. The letter of 1 John opens with a plea for honesty. It's a needed reminder that God wants us to be honest in our relationship with him. We don't have to pretend or lie; we can come honestly before God and be real. Stress that truth to the youth and let them comment on it.

2. Discuss the following questions: Can we honestly express our feelings about God to one another, or do we feel we always have to be "theologically correct"? What can we do to become more honest and real as a group? What should we do when we have questions and doubts?

Prayer

Thank you, God, for loving us as we are. Thank you that we don't have to play games with you. Forgive us when we feel the need to play charades or denial or any of the other games Christians sometimes play. Help us to be honest with you and honest with each other. Amen.

LOVING PEOPLE: GETTING PERSONAL

Focal Text—1 John 3:11-24

Learning Goal

The purpose of this session is to help youth understand that love for others is always specific and personal. John stresses this several times in 1 John, and our focal passage includes a verse that says, "Let us love, not in word or speech, but in truth and action" (3:18). This session will challenge youth to notice specific people and to show them personal love.

Introducing the Session

1. Begin the session by reading, or having one of the youth read, Matthew 22:24-40. Point out that Jesus reduced all the commandments to two primary truths: love God and love people. Remind the youth that last week we looked at the first of those two truths—how to love God. Review some of the highlights of that study on "Loving God: The Games Christians Play."

2. This week we look at the second of those two truths—how to love people. John hits this note several times in our focal passage. Have the youth read 1 John 3:11, 14, 16, 18, and 24. By the time they have finished reading those verses, the youth will get the point: loving others is crucial to our faith, and we can't love God if we don't love people.

Exploring the Text

1. Explain that John's insistence that we love others is an echo of what he heard Jesus say. John had walked and talked with Jesus and learned about love directly from Jesus. He even referred to himself as "the one Jesus loved." Recap Jesus' life and ministry—how he focused on a few people and loved them in tangible ways. When it came to loving others, Jesus didn't think big; he thought small.

2. Propose the idea that every person we know has an invisible "love tank." If a person's love tank is full, he or she will thrive emotionally and physically. But if that person's love tank gets low or empty, he or she will likely have some major problems. Our calling, as followers of Christ, is to fill those love tanks.

Discuss

• Think of the people in your life who mean the most to you. What would you say about their love tanks? Are they most often full, empty, or somewhere in between? What could you do to keep them full?

• Think of your own love tank. What would you say about it? Is it most often full, empty, or somewhere in between? What could others do to help you keep it full?

3. Ask the youth why we don't do a better job of filling people's love tanks and let them give reasons why love is so scarce in many of our relationships. Then suggest two reasons we don't love the way these verses tell us to love: (1) we forget how crucial our love is to others, and (2) we get busy and unintentionally neglect the people around us. Forgetfulness and busyness always sabotage real love.

4. Read the following quotes from Paula D'Arcy and Thomas Keating and discuss them with the youth:

> The formula for finding your own, primary mission is here: Put down this book. Walk outside your house, trailer, or apartment. Look in through a window. Now you see where Christ has sent you. Serving starts where you are. If you understand that your mission to the faces at your table, no matter how few, ranks in importance with the mission of a great evangelist to crowds of thousands, then you have begun to understand Love. (Paula D'Arcy, *Where the Wind Begins*)

> When Mother Teresa picked up a dying man in the streets of Calcutta, she captured the imagination of the world. It was a striking symbol of God's concern for the poor. Each of us is surrounded by opportunities. We don't have to be invited to the United Nations or go to a summit conference to save the world. Divine love suggests a first step that needs to be taken here and now. (Thomas Keating, *Reawakenings*)

Discuss

• What do these two quotes have in common?

• What seems difficult about showing love to other people in these ways? How could we overcome such difficulties?

• How can we minister to "the faces at our table"—that is, how can we be more loving to our parents, brothers and sisters, and close friends? Why is this important?

Closing the Session

1. Though we often feel as if the Bible is hard to understand, its call to us, according to Jesus, is to love God and love people. We don't have to be theologians or Bible scholars to understand the meaning of Scripture. This session has helped us consider how we can be faithful to the second of those truths—loving the people in our lives.

2. Refer again to the Paula D'Arcy quote and ask the youth these questions: Are there specific people in your family who need your focused love? Are there people at school who need you to fill their love tanks? Are there people in our youth group who need you to be more loving and attentive to them? Who are the people God is calling you to love in a personal, tangible way?

Prayer

Dear God, we talk a lot about love, but we're not particularly good at loving the people around us. Forgive us when we forget how important it is to fill love tanks, and forgive us when we get so busy and distracted that we fail to notice the people around us. Help us to be more like Jesus, who gave himself unreservedly to seeing and loving the people in his life. In his name and spirit, we pray. Amen.

FOLLOWING JESUS: GETTING A NEW LIFE MAP

Focal Text—1 John 5:18-21

Materials: Roadmap (or phone with Google map), globe or map that shows outdated country names or divisions

Learning Goal

In this session, we lead youth to consider ways that following Jesus makes them nonconformists. In 1 John 5, John ends his letter by discussing the difference Jesus makes in a person's life. One of those differences is that he gives a person a completely new life map. This session will challenge youth to look at their own life maps and to see if it needs to be updated to conform to the way of Christ.

Introducing the Session

1. Review the first two sessions, reminding the youth that we have been studying 1 John. So far, we have looked at what John had to say about loving God and loving people, the key components in what Jesus called "the Great Commandment." Ask the youth what they remember about those first two sessions.

2. Ask for volunteers to read 1 John 5:18-21. Encourage the youth to notice the three things John says we can *know* in 1 John 5:18-21. First, we *know* that those who have real faith do not habitually and intentionally sin (5:18). Second, we *know* that those who have real faith are on a countercultural journey that makes them different from others (5:19). Third, we *know* that those who have real faith accept that Jesus has given them a new understanding of life (5:20).

3. Hold up a roadmap (or pull up Google maps on your phone). Talk about the ways we use maps—to find directions to where we want to go, to look up the

closest restaurant or movie theater or grocery store, to plan a road trip point by point, etc. Explain that we could also imagine having "life maps" on which we plot the path of our lives—the big events that may change our course, the people we encounter, the big and small choices we make each day.

Tell them that in this session, we will think specifically about the second two things John says we can *know*: being different and getting a new understanding of life. John is saying here that Christians are given a new life map when they decide to follow Jesus.

4. Ask the youth if they know what the acronym WWJD means. If not, note that it stands for the question, "What would Jesus do?" and was made popular in the 1990s as people reflected on ideas in Charles Sheldon's 1896 book *In His Steps: What Would Jesus Do*. The letters appeared on all kinds of items, from bracelets to t-shirts. Though the trend faded, the question is still key. We Christians try to figure out what Jesus would do in any given situation. Then we do our best to do what he would do.

Exploring the Text

1. Use the material in the teacher's guide to discuss the word *mathetes* (pronounced math-ay-**teez**). Then tell the youth about the Sermon on the Mount in Matthew 5–7, where Jesus lays out the specifics of a life that is dedicated to following him. That sermon is really a new map for living life in Christ, and it shows us the journey we should take. Ask the youth what they know about the Sermon on the Mount and then tell them some of the issues Jesus addresses in that sermon. It's a crash course in Christian Living 101.

Discuss
• How does following Jesus make a person different from others?
• Do you ever feel like an outcast because of your faith?
• How can you share who you are in Jesus at school and with your friends?
• Do you ever feel embarrassed to call yourself a Christian? If so, what do you do about this feeling?
• What specific things about following Jesus make it hard to do so?

2. John ends the letter of 1 John by telling his readers to keep themselves from idols. Idols can be anything that keeps us from serving God.

Discuss

• What are some of the idols that we try to serve today (popularity, wealth, success, approval, grades, etc.)?
• How do these keep us from following the life map Jesus has drawn for us?
• What steps can you take to follow the path on your life map as a Christian?

Closing the Session

1. If available, show an outdated globe or map to the group. If you don't have one, you can at least tell them that maps and globes have changed dramatically in the past thirty years. Countries like the Soviet Union, East Germany, Czechoslovakia, Yugoslavia, Tibet, and South Vietnam have disappeared, and others like Croatia, Slovenia, Lithuania, Moldova, Latvia, and Kosovo have become nations. As we live for Christ and try to be his *mathetes*, we need to be updating our life maps frequently—making sure they align with what Jesus did and taught. This is what it means to "grow as a Christian."

2. Since this is the last session from 1 John, recap the three main takeaways from our study of the book: (1) loving God by not playing games but instead being honest and real, (2) loving others by focusing on the people around us and doing tangible things to affirm and help them, and (3) letting Christ give us a new life map and becoming serious about following that map.

Prayer

God, thank you that there are things we can *know* because of your word in the Bible and because of Jesus' example. Help us follow the life map Jesus gives us by daring to be different and by sharing our new understanding of life. Show us the things that we've made into idols, and guide us to put them in their proper place as we learn to love you and love others more and more. Amen.

LEARNING TO LEAD: WHO'S IN CHARGE HERE?

Focal Text—3 John

Learning Goal

This final session focuses on 3 John and leads youth to think about leadership. The short letter of 3 John addresses a leadership issue in the early church and describes two distinct leadership styles. As they study this letter, the youth will have opportunity to think about the people who lead them, but they will also get to consider the kind of leaders they are now and the kind of leaders they will become in the future.

Introducing the Session

1. Take a moment to tell the youth that the little books of 2 and 3 John and Jude are about bad religion. Second John is about *bad teaching*. Third John is about *bad leadership*. And Jude is about *bad living*. You might want to reread the material in the teacher's guide on these three letters and highlight the main truths in each one.

2. This study will focus on 3 John, a letter of only fifteen verses. It was probably that short so it would fit on one page of papyrus and could be circulated easily among early church members.

3. Describe the situation that prompted the writing of the letter. A group of traveling prophets was coming to the church, and John wanted the church to show hospitality to these visitors. Evidently, not everyone in the church wanted to welcome these guests, so John wrote the letter to weigh in on the debate. In the process, he gives us a look at two contrasting styles of leadership.

Exploring the Text

1. The letter introduces us to three men: Gaius, Diotrephes, and Demetrius. Gaius is a leader in the church John is writing to, Diotrephes is a heavy-handed member of that church who doesn't want to welcome the visiting prophets, and Demetrius is either another church member or the leader of the visiting prophets. Let's meet these three characters.

2. *(As the Scripture is read for each character, consider listing the names on a dry-erase board and having the youth call out characteristics for each man. Write the characteristics beneath the names.)* First, let's meet Gaius, "Mr. Hospitality." Have someone read verses 1-8, which describe Gaius as one who loves the truth and one who has been hospitable to guests in the past. He is either the pastor of the church John is writing to or a key leader in that church. He is also the one who must help the church consider how to treat these visiting prophets.

3. Next, let's meet Diotrephes, "Mr. Intimidator." Have someone read verses 9-10, where John describes Diotrephes as one who (1) has an ego problem, (2) is authoritarian, (3) is critical of others, and (4) is inhospitable and unfriendly. His leadership style was marked by intimidation and domination. It's a style that is still prominent in our schools, churches, businesses, and government.

4. Finally, let's meet Demetrius, "Mr. Dependable." Have someone read verses 11-12, where John describes Demetrius as (1) a good, dependable person, (2) one who has the support of the church, and (3) a person of truth. It's obvious that John prefers Demetrius to Diotrephes and hopes the church will follow his style and emulate his spirit. He embodies a completely different leadership style, one marked by submission and servanthood.

5. Then John closes his brief letter. Have someone read verses 13-15 and suggest that a bigger issue lies at the heart of 3 John than how the church would treat visiting prophets. The letter is really about leadership and the kind of church the people wanted to have. Did they want a Diotrephes kind of church that was heavy on rules, threats, and domination? Or did they want a Demetrius kind of church that was heavy on consensus, grace, and submission?

Closing the Session

1. Help the youth think about the session by asking questions like these:

Discuss

• Have you seen these two styles of leadership? Can you give examples of each?
• Which style worked best? How and why?
• Is our church a Diotrephes church or a Demetrius church?
• As you think about your own leadership style, are you Diotrephes or Demetrius?
• What can our church do to be more hospitable and welcoming to outsiders the way that Gaius was?

2. Third John reminds us of several truths: (1) the church has never been perfect, (2) leadership means different things to different people, and (3) making outsiders feel welcome has been an issue in the church from the very beginning. Encourage the youth to continue taking part in church and thinking of ways they can be leaders. Remind them that they are never too young to make a difference.

Prayer

Thank you, God, for our church and its leaders. Give them wisdom and grace as they lead us. And give us wisdom and grace, too, when we have opportunities to be in leadership positions. We pray this in the name of Jesus Christ, our best model of leadership. Amen.

TEACHING 1, 2, 3 JOHN AND JUDE TO CHILDREN

INTRODUCTION

Throughout 1, 2, and 3 John, John is clear about one thing: the people are children of God. And as children of God, they are called to live in specific ways. As children of God, we too are called to live in specific ways. But how do we do this, and how can we teach it to children?

In session 1, "Being Children of God," you and your class will participate in activities that help you explore the light and the darkness. According to 1 John, being children of God means that we walk in the light. God is in the light, and to be children of God, we must walk in the light with God. By trying to walk through an obstacle course in the dark and painting with glow paint, children will learn what it means to walk in the light and why it is important. They will also learn that being children of God means following God's commandments. In the reflection activity for session 1, they will learn that some rules are helpful to follow and others are commands from God.

Part of being children of God is following the command to love others, but what does "love" mean? Session 2, "How Do We Love?" focuses on what it means to love others. Love is more than hearts and hugs; Scriptures like 1 John and other passages can help you teach children that love is an action. When we

---

Jessica Asbell serves as the minister to children at First Baptist Church of Roswell, Georgia. She has worked with children in various capacities at several churches, including Winter Park Baptist in Wilmington, North Carolina; First Baptist of Decatur, Georgia; and Highland Hills Baptist in Macon, Georgia. She has a Master of Divinity from McAfee School of Theology and a BBA from Mercer University. In her spare time she loves to read, watch movies, and spend time with her sweet kitty, Lucy.

show others we love them, we do more than simply tell them. We show love
by helping when people need it, by encouraging them, and by seeing the spark
of God in them. From the opening activity in which children help each other
succeed to the reflection activity where they pack toiletry items and food for the
homeless, children will learn what it means to love others. Their memory verse
will remind them that we love others because love comes from God. God loves
everyone; as children of God, we are to love everyone too.

Session 3 focuses on "The Truth about Our Faith." From singing "My God
Is So Big" to playing "Which Is More Powerful?" children will learn that God
is mightier than anything else, including the strongest man in the world! They
will learn that their faith can be mighty too—that through our faith we can
be stronger than the most powerful hate. Children will also learn that we have
proof of how powerful God's love is. The Holy Spirit declares it, and the Holy
Spirit does not lie. Jesus' baptism declares it. And Jesus' death and resurrection
declare it. Through exploring the Bible passage, children will be reminded that
they can always trust God to tell the truth.

Session 4 helps answer the question, "How Should We Live?" It focuses on
2 and 3 John and Jude. In 2 and 3 John, John reiterates that we should keep
God's commands and love one another. And all three short books teach us that
we should live by loving one another, living according to God's commandments, being on our guard, walking in the truth, supporting other Christians,
and imitating what is good. By playing Simon Says, children will start to
understand the need to differentiate what the world tells us to do and what God
tells us to do. By playing a game called "Fact or Fiction?" children will recognize that some things that seem true may not be, and some things that seem a
bit fantastical are true. In this lesson, children will learn what it means to walk
in the truth and be on guard against people who may lie to them, whether on
purpose or accidentally. They will also write their own letter to someone, telling
them how God wants them to live.

Each of these sessions includes a snack that is connected to the lesson. **If
you plan to serve the snack options, be sure to check for food allergies first.**

As children learn what it means to be children of God, how to love, the
truth about our faith, and how they should live, they will develop a better
understanding of who God is and how God wants them to live.

Session Outline

BEING CHILDREN OF GOD

Focal Text—1 John 1:1–3:10

WELCOME

Greet children with a smile and a welcome as they come into Bible study. Make sure they know that you're happy to be there with them!

OPENING ACTIVITY: TRYING TO WALK IN THE DARK

Before the Session: Use chairs and other items to create an obstacle course in an area that is separate from your classroom, if possible. Bring a blindfold.

Ask, "How many of you have ever tried to walk around a dark room? Did you run into something? Did you step on a toy?" *(Allow time for responses.)* Explain that it's hard to know where we're going when we can't see anything. Today we will find out how good everyone is at walking in the dark.

Turn off the light. Choose a volunteer to walk through the obstacle course you created. Blindfold that child and tell everyone to be quiet and not give hints. Next, ask someone to call out directions to the child who is blindfolded. Finally, take off the blindfold and have the child walk through the obstacle course with the light on. Allow each child to participate if desired.

Questions

• Was it hard to do the obstacle course blindfolded and without help?
• Was it easier to do the obstacle course with someone calling out directions?
• How did you feel when you walked the obstacle course without the blindfold?

Close the activity by reading 1 John 1:5-7 to your class. Talk about how God is light and helps us know where to go and what to do.

ACTIVITY: PAINTING WITH GLOW IN THE DARK PAINT

Before the Session: Gather these supplies—enough blank paper for each person to have two sheets; glow-in-the-dark paint (or use lemon juice and a black light); paintbrushes; glow-in-the-dark stars; lamp

Explain that today the children get to paint, but this paint is special because it glows in the dark (if using lemon juice, tell them this paint is invisible but will glow in the black light). It's hard to see the paint with the lights on, but when we turn them off, they will be able to see what they painted.

Give each child two sheets of paper and access to paint and paintbrushes. On the first sheet, have the kids paint the word "love" using glow paint (or lemon juice). Then have them place their finished papers under the lamp to "charge." On the second sheet, allow them to paint anything they want (as time allows). After a few minutes, have them collect their painted papers from under the lamp.

Turn off the lights (if using lemon juice, turn on the black light) and remind the group that they couldn't really see their pictures when the lights were on. But now that the lights are off, they can clearly see the word "love." They can also see the other pictures they made.

Show them the glow-in-the-dark stars and note that they are like the paint: they aren't bright when the lights are on, but in the darkness they shine. Tell the kids that the glow paint and the stars have something else in common: they both need light first. To glow in the darkness, they have to charge under the light. Once they are charged, they shine brightly.

Explain that people are the same way. We don't really glow in the dark, but God's love charges our lives. It fills us so that we can share that love with others. Our world can be a dark place. Sometimes people do terrible things, and a lot of people don't know God. They walk in darkness because they don't have God's love to light the way. Those of us who know God walk in the light with God, and we receive God's love. And like the glow paint and the stars, we can shine brightly with God's love. *(Hold up one of the sheets that says "love.")* We can share

God's love with others and be a light for them. We can show people God's light and God's love. *(If desired, give each child a glow star to take home. Encourage them to put it somewhere in their rooms to remind them to be a light for God.)*

THE BIBLE PASSAGE: GOD IS LIGHT

Read 1 John 1:5-10; 2:3-11; and 3:1 from an easy-to-understand translation like the Contemporary English Version (CEV) or the Common English Bible (CEB).

Then explain the passage to the children by saying something like this:

God is light. That means God is good. There's not a trace of darkness in God. We can say that we are living for God, but what happens if we never read the Bible, never go to church, never talk to God, are mean to other people, take things that don't belong to us, lie to others, and ignore what God tells us to do? Are we really following God? *(Allow responses.)*

That's what John means by stumbling around in the dark. God is a light for our lives; God shows us the right way to go and the right thing to do. The book of Psalms reminds us that God's word is a lamp to our feet and a light for our path (Ps 119:105). We walk in the light when we do what God tells us to do. Sometimes we choose to do the wrong thing. We aren't perfect, but God will always forgive us. First John tells us that we can know if we're living for God. We know that we are living for God if we keep God's commandments. Let's find out what God's commandments are.

REFLECTION ACTIVITY: WHICH COMMANDMENT?

Tell the group that 1 John says we know we're living for God if we keep God's commandments. Explain that some rules are good to follow, and others are actual commandments from God. Play a game to see if the kids can tell which rules are from God. If the rule is from God, they should stand up and clap. If it's just a regular rule for everyday life, they can stay seated and quiet.

1. Clean your room.
2. Honor your father and mother. (God's commandment)

3. Don't lie. (God's commandment)
4. Eat all your dinner.
5. Feed your pets.
6. Only worship God. (God's commandment)
7. Don't steal. (God's commandment)
8. Brush your teeth.
9. Don't want what someone else has. (God's commandment)
10. Help someone get up when they fall.
11. Love your neighbor as you love yourself. (God's commandment)
12. Love God with all your heart, soul, mind, and strength. (God's commandment)

Remind the kids that these actions are good, but not all of them are things that God has commanded us to do. This means God orders us to do these things. As followers of God, we must do them. Maybe the children's mom or dad tells them they must clean their rooms before they can do anything else. That's a command from their parents. It's something they must do; there's no getting out of it. In the same way, God tells us to do certain things, and we know that we are following God when we do those things.

SNACK TIME

Before the Session: Get Golden Oreos and Original Oreos. As a healthier option, provide green apples and purple grapes or strawberries and blueberries.

Emphasize that we've been talking about light and darkness. For snack, we have something light and something dark. Assure the kids that chocolate, grapes, or blueberries aren't bad because they are dark, but the different shades of the food can help us remember our Bible study theme. As the children enjoy their snack, talk about ways we can share God's love with others and how we can let God's light shine through us.

MEMORY VERSE ACTIVITY: MISSING WORDS

Before the Session: Make copies of the worksheet on the following page so that each child can have one. Provide pencils if desired.

Memory Verse: "See what kind of love the Father has given to us in that we should be called God's children, and that is what we are!" (1 John 3:1a, CEB)

Give each child a worksheet, and note that there are some words missing in the memory verse. Tell them to look in the light from the flashlight and work together to figure out where the words go. Read the verse out loud (or ask a volunteer to read it) until you come to the first blank. Help the children determine which word fits there. Do this until all the words are filled in, and then recite the verse together.

MISSING WORDS

Some of the words have fallen out of our memory verse! Use the words in the light from the flashlight to fill in the rest of the verse. When all the words are filled in, read it out loud together.

See what kind of _____ the Father has _____ to us in that we _____ be _____ God's _____, and that is _____ we are! (1 _____ 3:1a, CEB)

love	called
should	what
of	children
given	John

HOW DO WE LOVE?

Focal Text—1 John 3:11–4:21

For this lesson, consider requesting ahead of time that parents donate items for the activity "How Do We Love?"

WELCOME

Greet children with a smile and a welcome as they come into Bible study. Make sure they know that you're happy to be there with them!

ACTIVITY: RELAY RACE

Before the Session: Prepare 16 inflated balloons or 16 beanbags, and gather 4 large tubs (if using balloons) or 4 medium-sized buckets (if using beanbags). Place 2 tubs filled with 8 balloons each (or 2 buckets with 8 beanbags each) on one side of the room, and place the empty tubs/buckets at the other end.

Tell the children that today we are learning how to show love to other people. One of the ways we can show love is by helping each other. Invite them to play a game where they team up and help one another.

Divide the kids into two teams. If your group is older, guide them to pass one balloon/beanbag down the line of teammates until it reaches the front of the line. That person will run to the tub/bucket and put the item in. Then they will go to the back of the line, get the next balloon/beanbag, and pass it down the line. The game continues until all items from the container one side of the room have been transferred to the container on the other side. The first team to finish wins. For younger or smaller groups, you could have everyone line up in front of the container and see how fast they can get all the balloons/beanbags into it. Time them and let them know how long it took.

Congratulate the kids on being such great helpers, even if their team wasn't the first to finish. Explain that they all did a good job passing the item to each other (or working together to fill a container) and were encouraging. Part of showing others we love them is helping them and working together.

THE BIBLE PASSAGE: GOD LOVES THE WORLD

Read 1 John 3:16-18, 4:7-13, 20-21 from an easy-to-understand translation like the Contemporary English Version (CEV) or the Common English Bible (CEB).

Then explain the passage to the children by saying something like this:

John reminds us that none of us are born loving God. A caring person brought you to church today so you can learn to love God. But guess what? God doesn't have to learn about you to love you. God has always loved you! God created you and already knows everything about you. He knows the things you do right and the things you do wrong. He knows how many hairs are on your head and how many loose teeth you have. He knows every cut and scrape and how you got them. God knows everything about you and loves you!

In fact, God loves us so much that before any of us were born, before the billions of people on our planet right now were born, God sent Jesus for us so that we could always be friends with God. God's love is perfect. Our love isn't. Sometimes we are mean to the people we love. Sometimes our friends hurt us and we don't love them anymore. Sometimes things happen and we stop talking to someone we used to love. But God's love is perfect.

Sometimes, though, God's love is hard to feel. Can you feel God giving you a hug? Can you see God? *(Allow responses.)* John reminds us that it's important to love our neighbors—that means the other people around us. We can see our neighbors and show love to them. And by showing love to our neighbors, by helping others and listening to them and being kind, we show love to God. John says we can't love God and hate our neighbor. To love God, we have to love others too.

Questions

• What are some ways that others have helped you?
• What are some ways that you have helped others?
• How can you help others this week?

REFLECTION ACTIVITY: HOW DO WE LOVE?

Before the Session: Collect the following items, either by asking parents for donations or setting up a donation box at your church: travel toiletry items (including toothbrushes and toothpaste), socks, bottled water, crackers, pouches of tuna, plastic utensils, napkins, cereal bars, fruit or applesauce cups, gallon Ziploc bags. Provide construction paper and markers, index cards, and tape. Make copies of the parent note at the end of this session to send home with each child.

Set up bag-packing stations. Separate the items into piles by type so the children can see each one clearly and be sure to include everything.

Tell the kids that we are learning how we should love others. In the book of 1 John, John talks a lot about how we can show love to other people. He makes it clear that showing love doesn't just mean saying, "I love you." In 1 John 3:17-18 he says, "if a person has material possessions and sees a brother or sister in need and that person doesn't care—how can the love of God remain in him? Little children, let's not love with words or speech but with action and truth" (CEB).

We should show people we love them by the things we do. How do they show love? *(Allow responses and include some of your own.)* Remind them that one of God's commandments that we talked about last week is to love our neighbor, which means loving all the people around us. First John reminds us that loving our neighbor means helping them. There are people who live in our city who are hungry. Some of them don't have a place to live and don't have the things they need to stay clean and healthy. They are our neighbors too. Encourage the children to help you make bags for these people. They can take the finished bags with them, keep them in the car, and (with adult supervision) hand them out to homeless and hungry people when they see them.

When each child has packed a few bags, invite them to make cards to put inside. They can write things like "God loves you," "I'm praying for you," and other encouraging notes. *(Tell the children that they can draw pictures and make designs, but they should not put their names on these cards for privacy reasons.)*

Be sure each child has a parent note to take home as well. This will explain the project to their caregivers.

Lead your class in prayer for the people who will receive the bags.

SNACK TIME

Before the Session: Prepare strawberries or heart-shaped cookies, and provide plates and napkins.

Remind the group that we've been learning about love. Love is more than just saying, "I love you." In fact, love is all about action. We can tell others we love them, but the best way is to show them by helping them, listening to them, and working together. Today's snack looks a bit like a heart. This heart reminds us to use our actions to show others that we love them. As the children eat, ask them to name ways that they can help others and show love this week.

MEMORY VERSE ACTIVITY: FIND AND UNSCRAMBLE THE VERSE

Before the Session: Write each word of the memory verse on a separate paper heart. Write the entire reference (1 John 4:7) on a heart as well. Hide the 23 hearts around the room.

Memory Verse: "Dear friends, let's love each other, because love is from God, and everyone who loves is born from God and knows God." (1 John 4:7, CEB)

Read the memory verse to the group. Explain that you've written each word of the verse on a heart and hidden all the hearts around the room. When you say "go," ask the kids to look for all 23 hearts and work together to put the memory verse together.

For younger children, you might write the verse on the board and help them put it together.

Older children can use their Bibles to unscramble the verse.

When they finish, give each child one of the hearts. Write the verse reference (or let the children write it) on the back of each heart to help them remember the memory verse.

As parents arrive, make sure the children take home the bags they packed. Give each parent a note to explain the ministry activity.

PARENT NOTE

Hi, parents!

Today we talked about what it means to show love to others—and how we show love not only by saying "I love you" but also by helping others. To that end, we have packed bags for the homeless. The bags include items such as travel-sized toiletries, a bottle of water, and various foods. Please leave these in your car, and when you see someone who looks hungry, give him or her a bag.

Thank you for helping us put our love into action!

Session 3

THE TRUTH ABOUT OUR FAITH

Focal Text—1 John 5

WELCOME

Greet children with a smile and a welcome as they come into Bible study. Make sure they know that you're happy to be there with them!

OPENING ACTIVITY: MY GOD IS SO BIG

Before the Session: Find the words and/or music to the song "My God Is So Big" from Crazy Praise presented by Kid Jamz. A lyric video is available at https://www. youtube.com/watch?v=Q320dTesx1c.

Rejoice with the children that God is so big and so mighty! Assure them there's nothing our God can't do. Today we are learning more about God and our faith. Invite them to learn a song about how God is more powerful than anything else. Use the following motions to help teach the song:

Refrain (sing twice): My God is so big *(stretch hands out)*, so strong and so mighty *(make muscle arms)*
there's nothing *(shake head)* my God cannot do *(clap clap)*.

The mountains *(put hands together above head to form a mountain peak)* are His, the rivers *(weave hands in and out to mimic a river's flow)* are His, the stars *(point to sky)* are His handiwork too.

Refrain

Once the children know the song, have them sing it in different ways (such as with loud voices, in whispers, etc.).

Thank them for praising God with you. Tell them this song is a wonderful reminder that God made everything and can do anything. Jesus tells us in Matthew 19:26 that nothing is impossible for God.

ACTIVITY: WHICH IS MORE POWERFUL?

Ask the group if they think there's anything or anyone more powerful than God. Offer some options and see how they answer.

- The strongest wrestler ever was Mark Henry, who pulled two tractor trailers at the same time (http://www.thesportster.com/wrestling/top-20-strongest-wrestlers-of-all-time/). Who is stronger, God or a wrestler?
- The world's strongest man was Louis Cyr, who lived in the late 1800s and early 1900s. He lifted 500 pounds with one finger and backlifted 4,337 pounds (https://en.wikipedia.org/wiki/Louis_Cyr). Who is stronger, God or the world's strongest man?
- An elephant's trunk can lift up to 770 pounds (http://www.realclearscience.com/blog/2013/10/the-most-amazing-appendage-in-the-world.html). Who is more powerful, God or an elephant?
- A hippo can weigh up to 8,000 pounds (http://www.animalfactguide.com/animal-facts/hippopotamus/). Who is bigger, God or a hippo?
- Hurricane Wilma, which happened in Cuba in 2005, was a category 5 hurricane—the worst category. It had winds of 175 miles per hour (https://weather.com/storms/hurricane/news/strongest-hurricanes-most-intense-atlantic-hurricanes-20130911#/10). Which is more powerful, God or a hurricane?
- The worst tornado recorded was the Tri-State Tornado, an F5 that had winds of 260+ mph. It happened in 1925 in Missouri, Illinois, and Indiana (http://www.cnn.com/2013/01/30/us/deadliest-tornadoes/index.html). Which is stronger, God or a tornado?
- Every living thing on the earth will die one day. Which is more powerful, God or death?

What other things can the kids think of that are strong or powerful? Admit to them that some of the ones on the list were silly. God is certainly more powerful than the strongest man alive or a hippo or even an elephant. But tornados and hurricanes are very powerful. They can hurt a lot of people and take down houses and trees. Sometimes when storms happen, we get scared. When you are afraid of a storm, always remember that God is more powerful than anything else. God is even more powerful than death. When Jesus died, he defeated death so that we can always be friends with God. Part of what we are learning today is that our faith is powerful too. And God's love is more powerful than anything else. In fact, in 1 John, John says that our faith in God's love and power can conquer the world—it can beat anything else! When you have faith in God, you are always on the winning team. It's doesn't always feel like it, but God's love will win in the end. (As children respond, thank them for their answers. Talk about how God is stronger and more powerful than any of those things.)

THE BIBLE PASSAGE: TRUSTING GOD

Read 1 John 5:1-15 from an easy-to-understand translation like the Contemporary English Version (CEV) or the Common English Bible (CEB).

Then explain the passage to the children by saying something like this:

John says that anyone who believes in Jesus is a child of God. Over the last few weeks, we've talked about how to know that we are children of God. We are children of God if we if we do what God says to do and if we love other people by helping them and showing that we care.

Today, we are learning that another part of being children of God is believing in Jesus. Our faith—our trust in God—is powerful. Sometimes things are hard in our world. Bad things happen and we don't understand why. But even then, we can remember that God's love is more powerful than anything else, and God will always be with us.

We have proof that these things are true. The Holy Spirit tells us they are true. This Spirit is a special gift from God. It is the voice or feeling inside of us that helps us feel closer to God and understand things about God. And the Holy Spirit does not lie! Also, when Jesus was baptized in the water, God said, "This is my Son." Jesus' baptism also tells us these things are true. Finally, Jesus' death on the cross and his resurrection—when he came back to life out of the tomb—tell us that these things are true. We have so much proof that God's love is more powerful than anything else and that God will always be with us!

Do you believe your parents/family members/teachers/church leaders when they tell you something? Most of you would probably answer yes, because you know that these people will tell you the truth. And if you can trust them, imagine how much more you can trust God to tell you the truth! God created the universe. God made you and me and everything around us. We can trust God to tell us the truth. We can trust God's Spirit, the Holy Spirit, to tell us the truth. And we can trust God's Son, Jesus, to tell us the truth. Knowing and believing these things changes our lives! We know that we are loved no matter what. And we know that we will get to be God's friend forever. When bad things happen, we can trust that God's love will win.

REFLECTION ACTIVITY: SHARING JESUS WITH OTHERS

Before the Session: For the game, prepare at least 1 piece of 11x17 paper per child or 1 carpet square per child. The object of the game is to get everyone from one side of the room to the other by sharing Jesus with each other.

Remind the group that the Holy Spirit says we can have eternal life through Jesus. We can live forever with God one day! We can trust that this is true. Because of God's great love for us, God wants us to help each other and share the love of Jesus with those around us. Let's play a game to help us do that.

Invite the group to pretend that the floor of the room is a rushing river. Encourage them to work together to build a "bridge" to cross it. They should not let their feet touch the bare floor. The goal of the game is to show Jesus' love by helping each other.

Ask all the children to form a line at one end of the room. Give each child a piece of paper or a carpet square. When you say "go," the first person in line will put his square on the floor in front of him and stand on it. The next person will step onto the first person's square with him, say "Jesus loves you," and then put her own square in front of the first square and stand on it. Then the third person in line will step onto the first square, say "Jesus loves you" to that child, step on the second square, say "Jesus loves you" to that child, and then put his own square on the floor in front of the second square and stand on it. The game will continue in this way until the "bridge" of squares stretches across the room and every child is standing on a square. At that point, the first child will pick up his square and walk across the entire bridge, stopping on each person's square and saying "Jesus loves you" until he reaches the other side of the river. The second child will do the same, and so on, until the entire group has made it to the opposite shore and the bridge has been removed. As time allows, they can play the game again to get back to where they started.

Compliment the way the kids worked together. Tell them that sometimes life is hard. People get sick, storms come and destroy property, children are hungry, and individuals are sad or lonely. In times like that, followers of Jesus can show love by helping in many ways. Just like the group worked together to build a bridge over the rushing river and expressed how much Jesus loved all of them, they can work together to share Jesus' love with others in their daily lives. Remind them that because we believe Jesus is God's Son and gives us eternal life, we allow him to change us to be more like God. They don't have to be grownups to share the love of Jesus!

SNACK TIME

Before the Session: If you know some of your children's favorite snack foods, bring those to class. If you don't, provide popular snacks like goldfish, chocolate chip cookies, etc., along with plates and napkins

As the children eat, ask them to share about their favorite foods. Talk about how we like to tell others about our favorite things: our favorite TV shows, movies, books, and games. We like to tell others about our favorite candy, snack, and meal. Just like we love to tell others about our favorite things, we also should love to tell others about Jesus. We should love to tell them about the things Jesus does in our lives and how God's love changes us. When we talk about those things, we are sharing our faith with others.

MEMORY VERSE ACTIVITY:
GO AND TELL RELAY RACE

Before the Session: Before class, write each word of the memory verse on an index card. Make 2 sets of cards, 1 set for each team. Also bring a roll of tape to class.

Memory Verse: "God gave eternal life to us, and this life is in his Son." (1 John 5:11b, CEB)

Divide the class into two teams. Give each team one set of cards. Ask a helper to put a rolled piece of tape on the back of each card so it will stick to the wall.

Tell the group that God wants us to share the love of Jesus with others. We can tell people about the eternal life God gives us—that one day we can all live forever with God. Invite them to do a relay race to help them learn the memory verse. Tell them to be sure each child has an index card. (If you don't have enough cards, play the game more than once so that every kid gets a chance; or, if there are more cards than kids, some children can have more than one card.) When you say "go," team members should work together to put themselves in verse order, and then they should run one by one to the designated spot, tape their card to the wall, and run back so the next person can go. The first team to finish the verse in order and read it aloud wins. (For younger children, you could print the verse somewhere so they can easily get it in the right order.)

As parents arrive, thank the children for participating today.

HOW SHOULD WE LIVE?

Focal Text—2 and 3 John, Jude

WELCOME

Greet children with a smile and a welcome as they come into Bible study. Make sure they know that you're happy to be there with them!

OPENING ACTIVITY: SIMON SAYS

Before the Session: Bring a Bible to class.

Remind the group that last week we talked about our faith and God's awesome power. We learned that God is more powerful than anything else and that we are on the winning team. No matter what happens, God will never leave us. Today we will learn how to put our faith into practice and live as Christians. Sometimes it's hard to know which rules are God's rules and which rules are other people's rules.

Invite the group to play a game of Simon Says. Tell them you will give instructions, but they must listen for the important words, "Simon says." Only then should they do what you say. Lead them in a quick game to be sure they understand the rules: "Simon says jump up and down. Simon says stop. Turn in a circle." If anyone moved on the third instruction, they are out!

If possible, ask for volunteers to take turns being Simon. Remind them not to say "Simon says" every time, and encourage them to think of funny movements ("pull your ears," "pinch your nose," "make a pig noise," etc.).

After a few rounds, ask if they thought it was hard to know when to do something. Did anyone make a mistake and do what they were told to do when they didn't hear "Simon says"? Note that sometimes it's hard for us to follow

God's rules. We hear rules all the time, and sometimes it's hard to know which are "good rules" and which are God's rules. God doesn't say "Simon says"! But we do have something that helps us know God's rules. *(Hold up a Bible.)* God gave us the Bible so that we can know the rules to live by as followers of Jesus.

Can anyone tell us what rule we have learned about love? We know that God wants us to love one another. A few weeks ago, we talked about how loving others means more than just giving someone a hug or saying we love them. We show that we love each other through our actions. When we do things to help someone, we show them that we love them. When we listen to someone who is upset, we show them that we love them. When we make sure someone else has enough to eat, we show them that we love them. God doesn't want us simply to tell people that we love them. God sent Jesus to show how much God loves us. Because of Jesus, we can be with God forever! God wants us to show others we love them through our actions too.

ACTIVITY: FACT OR FICTION

Before the Session: Read over the list of fact or fiction below, or create your own list of weird but true facts plus false statements to read to the kids.

Tell the group that over the past three weeks we have read passages from 1 John and learned that we should love one another and follow God's rules. Today, we will read from three very short Bible books: 2 John, 3 John, and Jude. These books, which are actually letters, also talk about how we should live as followers of Jesus. Another important way to live is to tell the truth. We shouldn't lie to other people or about other people, but sometimes it's hard to know what's true and what's not.

Read the list of "facts," and ask the kids if they can guess which ones are true and which are not true (fiction). If they get it wrong, let them know and then explain why.

Fact or Fiction

1. Cheetahs can change direction in midair when chasing their prey (Fact)
2. A zebra has black and white striped skin. (Fiction. A tiger's skin is striped like his fur, but a zebra has black skin with striped fur.)

3. The sun is yellow. (Fiction. The sun is white.)

4. The eastern spotted skunk does a handstand before it sprays. (Fact)

5. Bats are the only mammals that fly. (Fact. Birds are not mammals.)

6. Cats communicate using at least sixteen "cat words." (Fact)

7. The Sahara Desert is the biggest desert on earth. (Fiction. Technically, Antarctica is the biggest desert on earth at 5.4 million square miles vs. the Sahara's 3.6 million. Deserts must be dry, inhospitable, and lacking in precipitation. They don't have to be sandy or hot.)

8. African elephants have ears shaped like the continent of Africa. (Fact)

9. Kangaroos don't hop backwards. (Fact)

10. Lightning never strikes the same place twice. (Fiction. The Empire State Building gets struck by lightning up to 100 times a year.)

Note: Facts from http://kids.nationalgeographic.com/explore/adventure_pass/weird-but-true/mammals/#WBT1600x9004.png and fiction from http://boredomtherapy.com/biggest-scientific-myths/.

THE BIBLE PASSAGE: LIVING THE WAY GOD WANTS

Read 2 John 4-6; 3 John 1-5, 9, 11, 12; and Jude 20-21 from an easy-to-understand translation like the Contemporary English Version (CEV) or the Common English Bible (CEB).

Then explain the passage to the children by saying something like this:

We just played a game and tried to figure out which sentences were facts and which were fiction. It wasn't easy! Sometimes it's hard to know what's true and what's not as we try to follow God. Even back in the days of the early church, this was hard for people, so some of Jesus' followers wrote letters to encourage them.

Second John is written to a "dear lady" who must have been important to John. He reminds her and her children to keep following God's command to love one another. He also tells them to be on their guard because some people don't believe in Jesus. In fact, during that time, some were saying things about Jesus that weren't true. These people knew what Jesus said, but they added things to it. They tried to give the people more rules to follow—more things they had to do to be loved by God. But they were wrong.

Third John is written to a man named Gaius, but John is also talking to the whole church. He reminds them to imitate what is good. When you imitate someone, you do what he or she is doing. *(Make a few funny faces or movements and get the kids to imitate you.)* A man named Diotrephes was causing trouble in the church. He ignored the directions John sent, and he told people the wrong thing. Third John reminds us that it's important to follow people who are doing the right thing—like Gaius and Demetrius. If we don't, it's easy to choose to do the wrong thing.

A man named Jude wrote the last letter. He encouraged people to fight for the faith. Sometimes people tell us the wrong thing about Jesus. But we should do what Jude says in verses 20-21: "build each other up . . . , pray in the Holy Spirit, keep each other in the love of God, wait for the mercy of our Lord Jesus Christ, who will give you eternal life."

Tell the kids that all four of the letters we have studied—1, 2, 3 John and Jude—help us know how we should live if we want to follow God. We should show love to one another, obey God's rules, be on guard against people who don't tell the truth, be truthful ourselves, help others, and do what is good. When we do these things, we will live the way that God wants us to live.

REFLECTION ACTIVITY: WRITING YOUR OWN LETTER

Before the Session: Gather enough paper, pencils/pens, markers/crayons for all the kids to have some.

For Older Children

Ask the kids to imagine they are writing a letter to someone to tell them how God wants them to live. This can be a person they know or someone they make up. Encourage them to use the letter to share ways that the person can show love to others and some of the rules God wants us to live by. They can add color to embellish their letters if they like.

For Younger Children

Ask the group to name some ways we can show love to others. Then ask them to name some of the rules God wants us to follow. Encourage them to draw and color ways we can show love to others and rules God wants us to live by.

As time allows, ask for volunteers to share their letters or pictures. If they wish, they can take them home and give them to someone.

SNACK TIME

Before the Session: Collect ingredients for trail mix—Chex cereal, Cheerios, mini marshmallows, M&Ms, small pretzels, and other suitable foods. Bring bowls for the ingredients, serving spoons or measuring cups, and resealable sandwich bags. Set up a station of bowls and spoons so that children can go down the line, adding food items to their bags.

For snack today, have the children wash their hands well. Then guide them to follow these directions to make their own trail mix:

1. Line up at the table.
2. When it's your turn, get a plastic bag.
3. Walk along the table, and choose which foods to put in your bag.
4. Only put one scoop of each food into the bag.
5. Seal your bag and return to your seat.

If more food remains after everyone finishes, you may decide to let them add more. Enjoy the snack together as a group. As they eat, ask them about the directions they have to follow in their lives. What happens when they miss a step? Why are rules and directions important?

MEMORY VERSE ACTIVITY: PLAY TELEPHONE

Memory Verse: "Whoever practices what is good belongs to God. Whoever practices what is bad has not seen God." (3 John 11b, CEB)

Ask the group to sit in a circle. Explain that to show them how we sometimes hear the wrong thing, we will play a game of Telephone to learn the memory verse. Whisper the verse to the person sitting on your right. Then that person should whisper it to the person beside her. Tell the kids to keep going around the circle until the verse gets to the person sitting on your left. That person says the memory verse out loud. See if the result is different from the actual verse!

As time allows, play a few rounds, mixing up the circle each time. At the end, lead everyone in saying the memory verse together.

As parents arrive, thank the children for participating today.

www.ingramcontent.com/pod-product-compliance
Lightning Source LLC
LaVergne TN
LVHW021500080426
835509LV00018B/2348